Pennies from
a Heav'n

Dear Grace,

Family and home is where the story begins
.... and continues.

Cherish those memories)

Mann
11-1-11

MARVIN JOSAITIS, PhD

Pennies from a Heav'n

THE JOY OF MAKING FAMILY

TATE PUBLISHING
AND ENTERPRISES, LLC

Published by Tate Publishing & Enterprises, LLC
127 E. Trade Center Terrace | Mustang, Oklahoma 73064 USA
1.888.361.9473 | www.tatepublishing.com

Tate Publishing is committed to excellence in the publishing industry. The company reflects the philosophy established by the founders, based on Psalm 68:11,
"The Lord gave the word and great was the company of those who published it."

Book design copyright © 2011 by Tate Publishing, LLC. All rights reserved.
Cover design by Kenna Davis
Interior design by Nathan Harmony

Published in the United States of America

ISBN: 978-1-61346-809-8
1. Biography & Autobigoraphy / General
2. Biography & Autobigoraphy / Personal Memoir
11.10.10

Acknowledgments

Inspired to write this book by Judd Mulvaney, a fictional character created by Joyce Carol Oates, I express my gratitude and appreciation to everyone who has contributed to the kaleidoscope, which follows. Most of the contributors no longer walk among us except through the essential gift of making family, their greatest gifts to me. I hope that I have contributed to extending their memories and their lives through a few more generations to follow. My greatest thanks goes to my wife and best friend, Donna, who inspires me to keep the music playing on forever.

Prologue

Kaleidoscopes are unique toys. Sir David Brewster invented them in 1816 while he was conducting experiments on the polarization of light. I was fascinated as a boy with this toy. I still am. Tubes; mirrors; loose, colored objects tumbling in arbitrary patterns; changing refractions; simply beautiful. *Kaleidoscope*: a fascinating word from the Greek *kalos* (beautiful) and *eidos* (shape) and *scopeo* (to look at or examine). Kaleidoscope—looking at beautiful forms.

I have realized for some time now that one's life, my life, is really a kaleidoscope. My waking hours and my dreams constantly flow from one to another in splendid kaleidoscopic forms, blending current reality and experience with reminiscences and past memories. And my

mind twists each beautiful moment into the ever present. Past becomes a new present, making me the sum
total of my experiences in its ebb and flow with the now.
The future is only what I meld between past and present,
going forward.

And so it goes on and on as I turn the kaleidoscope.
Flashes of events past become who I am today. Constant
flashes of memory mixed with new, current lights inter-
mingle, revitalizing who I have been into an ever-shaping
refractive who I am.

Flash!

Flash 1

During my sophomoric teenage period, I would laugh at my mother as we walked to the store. We had only one car, which my father took to work. But it didn't matter. With a car or not, our walks were moments of experiencing one another as well as the world about. I loved it. But there was Mom, always looking down as we walked. Looking always for pennies or the stray coin that had fallen from a previous traveler. I would laugh as she paused our conversation and pace to stoop down and pick it up—a mere penny.

"Mom, don't bother." I chuckled. "It's only a penny. And pennies are almost becoming a meaningless symbol of the past. They are nearly worthless. In fact, I think that the dime should become the least valuable coin in the realm." I puffed my chest with sophomoric pride.

With a tonality signaling a mixture of frustration and patient anger, she would burst forth: "Never forget, Marvin, that pennies make dollars. You may think it foolish now, but never forget." And so the moment would pass until our next walk, punctuated with the same dialogue at some point when the conversation and the pace paused to retrieve the copper treasure lying in wait.

Strange how often I now remember these moments past. As a man, my mother continued to ask me if I found any pennies that day. I would chuckle and respond as I had on our walks. She would remind me again, using her same words.

My mother died on December 13, 1994, just before her favorite time of year—Christmas. It was her favorite because as a girl with little financial wealth, she had the riches of a beautiful caring family. As the youngest of nine (actually eleven but two brothers had died) an older brother—Humphrey—bought her an artificial, cardboard Christmas tree with real candles. She would watch the candles until they had to be extinguished. And she would dream of worlds beyond her reach. Her mother, my Mimi (French Canadian for *grandmother*), had become a widow in her early fifties and had raised her six, unmarried children by cleaning homes and cooking part time. So pennies were those sovereigns that indeed became dollars.

And there I sat in a restaurant having a bit of breakfast, taking a break from sitting with my dying, comatose mother, readying to return to the hospital room for the last moments. "I'll Be Home for Christmas" was being crooned in the background as tears flowed down my cheeks. My all too brief forty-five years with a most endearing, barely five-foot-tall woman-mother-friend-confidant waltzed from memory to memory in three-quarters time, as my trusted handkerchief absorbed the last salty residue of our final chapter together. How often I remember it. *Never forget, I'll always be home for Christmas and whenever you need me.* And when I got up to pay my bill, I caught the glimmer of a penny, a bright penny on the floor. As I paused and stooped down, I thought of my mother who probably, in some way, was thinking of me, perhaps with the same kaleidoscope of dreams and memories creating her last, beautiful earthly memories of our walks together when we had only each other and the mystery of the treasures awaiting our journey.

During the past seventeen years, I would not be able to recount how many pennies and other coins have entered into my world by merely focusing on the pavement below. And they have emerged at the strangest, often most troubling moments. Very difficult moments sometimes were graced with several pennies. I would even find them in old drawers or in parking spots where, for no reason, I parked. And there they were waiting for me, reminding me of a dear love and her chiding me never to forget.

After I shared this story with my spouse and children, each of them has stumbled upon a penny frequently, usually when they need some sign that all is right with their worlds. My child who has had the most difficult times finds the most and gives a moment of thanks to her Mimi. Mom seems to always be home for Christmas, even in July.

Flash 2

In her remarkably compelling 1996 novel, entitled *We Were the Mulvaneys*, Joyce Carol Oates writes a moving narration of a dysfunctional family. In 2002, Joyce Eliason recreated the novel into an acclaimed screenplay for television. The characters are real and accurate portrayals of so many families. Narrated throughout by the youngest of four children, Judd Mulvaney, the story relives the progressive decline of an affluent, happy, and complex upstate New York family beset with tragedy and a spiraling decline due to its dysfunctional behavior in hiding rather than solving its problems. Near the end of the book, Judd, who is now an adult, finds himself in a quandary whether to return to his home for a reunion of relatives. The fractured memories of his youth are at once painful and defining; nonetheless, he decides to drive back to be with his family after many years of absence, daring himself to find some positive shred of value in that reunion. Her character revisits the family that is left because he has realized that, despite the difficulties they experienced together in his youth, his life was immensely influenced by his relations, faltering though they were. He helps to rebuild from ashes and ultimately grow from his family experiences.

During the reading of the novel and often since, I have bonded with the narrator, Judd, who was the baby of his family, just as I am. Throughout life, I have often discovered that the baby of the family has absorbed the memories of the family members, listening as each retold the events. In effect, the baby can become the historian and narrator of the family. In many ways, I have. Often I can't separate what are my own memories from those of my family relations. It strangely appears to me that there is a cloud or film between the real that I actually experienced and the real that I experienced through the memories I heard relived. Judd felt the same way.

In effect, it was the fictional character Judd who inspired me to write my family memories. As he pondered,

> For all of my childhood as a Mulvaney, I was the baby of the family. To be the baby of such a family is to know you're the last little caboose of a long roaring train. They loved me so, when they paid attention to me at all. I was like a creature dazed and blinded by intense, searing light that might suddenly switch off and leave me in darkness ... always it seemed, hard as I tried, I could

MARVIN JOSAITIS

never catch up with all their good times, secrets, jokes—their memories. What is a family, after all, except memories?[1]

And at the end of the day, that is what one has left... memories.

For me, a powerful moment occurred when Judd is struggling with his decision to go back to a family reunion and confront or remain and try to forget. At that moment, Joyce Carol Oates, in her persistence and faith and hope in the ultimate values inherent in family life, carefully and sensitively sages, "You never give such relationships a thought living them. To give a *thought*—to *take thought*—is a function of dissociation, distance. You can't exercise memory until you've removed yourself from memory's source."[2] It is the author's attestation that families are made by working on it; it is an active and constant creation from whoever is involved. And ultimately, we grow as individuals in finding out who we really are, what we believe, and what we stand for. Indeed, families create memories, and at the end of the day, that is what we have left—memories.

Flash 3

Families don't just happen. Families are made.

"Making family" is an apt phrase that I learned a couple of years ago in discussions with friends. "Making family" is a rich term that all families, but American families in particular, would be smart in adopting. We become family; we are not family. We become family by consciously spending the time that we have, the precious time, in a quality way with our spouses, partners, children, grandparents, siblings, relatives creating memories that act as building blocks for the lives we live. A person builds one block at a time, just as we learned with our first creative toys. We do this by doing together and being there when someone is in need. We do this by making gifts, not always buying them. Contemporary life emphasizes material things with passing wealth and glitzy, fading fame so much that family life sometimes suffers the ignominy of the dollar sign and the unimportant. And children in the process cry out for the really meaningful touch, or word, or hug, or time together with no strings attached.

The careful creating of memories as proposed by Judd can be enriched in a person's cache with the term "making family."

So it is that special "dates" should continue between spouses after they have been married. It is good also for children to see that their parents still love being with one another, one on one. I remember that my parents would simply stand up at times unannounced and dance to one of their favorite tunes on the radio. They didn't know it then, but they were "making family." Donna and I tried doing the same with our children and always let them know that we were the most important people in the relationship of family: we were their parents but also best friends and lovers at one and the same time. Additionally, we made sure that we lived the importance of each parent having special times or dates with each child one on one. And when our three children and their spouses, whom we refer to as our children as well, started having children, we indicated that we would spend a lot of time with our six grandchildren, just like their mimis and papas did with them to build memories and share our waning lives, but we would limit the material goods. This forms the richness of the term "making family."

The ultimate realization of "making family" occurs when parents or siblings die. These special members with

Marvin Josaitis

whom you and they "made family" take to the grave realities and memories that only they have kept within themselves. As the survivor, you have memories of making family that only you recall. And so it is that photographs and reminiscences remain, but the interpretation of those photographs and experiences as well as the memories as you interpret them are colored by your perceptions. The reality of "making family" becomes whole only in the combination of the joint memories of the living and the dead.

"Making Family" is a complex and beautiful reality, alive and mysterious at one and the same time. The kaleidoscope is never the same view for any two people. The beauty and the symmetry continue to evolve and build the family in varying degrees. What an addition to the concept of the kaleidoscope of life!

Flash 4

Nicknames are funny things. My Mimi—Edwidge Sauvé Girard—who lived with her youngest child and therefore with me, was a marvelous woman. What grandchild would say anything different? She was a short but large woman. Silver hair. A bosom haven for small children like me. I was privileged to be her last grandchild. I boast her best! She called me "Bubúne," (accent on the last syllable) which I am told is a French Canadian colloquial term for *baby*. I was that. Perhaps that explains why my father called me "Bubbins" as a little boy. Neither nickname stuck, probably fortunately. I woke up with her chasing me and my taunting (as is my predisposition): "You can't catch me." I can remember vividly doing this with her and ending the chase in her arms. I think that I slowed the pace on purpose for the comfort zone. She only thought she won; I knew definitely that I had.

My kaleidoscope often pictures my Mimi, a tough but soft woman, who was a peasant—a woman of the fields. With less than eight (and probably only four) years of formal education, she farmed with her family in southwestern Ontario until she met Noé Girard, my Pipi, who was several years her senior.

Edwidge Sauvé had married as a teenager and continued to farm with Pipi. They had ten children, one of whom died during their first twenty years of marriage after he fell climbing a walnut tree. In 1912, they piled their nine remaining children and whatever belongings could fit into a horse-drawn wagon and crossed the Detroit River on a barge into Michigan. Theirs was another immigrant tale of the first part of the twentieth century. Mimi was forty-six and Pipi fifty-four. I suspect that they had a few dollars with them but maybe only pennies. Perhaps that is where my mother discovered her fascination with the coin.

Marguerite (later changed to Margaret) Agnes Girard was the last child born to a forty-nine-year-old Edwidge and a fifty-seven-year old Noé in Detroit on February 28, 1915. Supporting his large family as a night watchman at the Ternstedt GM motor plant in southwest Detroit, two years later he died a victim of a very serious asthma condition. Another older son died a few years later in a tragic New Year's Eve accident crossing a train-track. And so this middle-aged, farm-girl widow without a farm, did what she knew best—cleaning and cooking part time for a few wealthy Grosse Pointe auto scions as well as

MARVIN JOSAITIS

the veterans at Detroit's Fort Wayne. Now, her Bubúne chased her to the game of catch-me-if-you can and then fell into her arms, the arms of the only grandparent he would ever know. What a catch!

Mimi's uniform was always a simple printed cotton house-dress, loosely fitted, permitting breathing-comfort for her large torso. In winter, she kept warm under a dark over-sized wool topcoat that nearly grazed the top of her laced black shoes. Silver—or was it white gold?—hair framed a high cheek-boned expressive face clearly reflecting a combination of her French Canadian ancestry augmented with touches of Scottish and Native American heritage. Mischievously, I ran my small fingers through her silky hair and pretended that the facial wrinkles were rivulets for my ten digital canoes. Every line on her face harbored stories and feelings earned during decades of tough living by an equally strong and persistent spirit. My Mimi.

The saddest moment as a four or five year old occurred just after my dad and mother had decorated our Christmas tree, giving Mimi and their two sons the honor of hanging special ornaments to finish the family event. Due to Mimi's excessive weight on aging wobbly legs, she fell into the tree, shattering the celebration as well as treasured ornaments collected over the years. We all cried as we clung to each other in a family hug. No angry word was spoken. My gentle and patient dad made sure first that Mimi was not injured, and then said calmly, "Don't worry, Mom, we will fix everything together as a family. We're just glad you weren't hurt."

A group hug gave us the energy and the will to redo a broken tree and to mend temporarily broken hearts. We did just that. Families are made by carefully working together in love when adversity occurs. And what memories and growth ensue!

I did have a nickname that stuck. Being the baby of a large family of four uncles, four aunts, their spouses, thirty first cousins—many of whom were older than my mother, who was the "Bubúne" of her family—and many second cousins older than me, I was "adopted" by many cousins as the baby to watch over. Two of my first cousins, one my godmother and one her sister—both more than ten years my senior—called me "Butch" because my parents had my hair cut in military-butch format, trying to thicken the fine hair. The latter never worked, but the nickname stuck. With pride today, my cousins Lois and Norma, their spouses, and their children know me and refer to me by no other name. Each were really the sisters that I never was privileged to have. Their children all called me "Uncle Butch."

The only child of mine who had a nickname other than the proverbial "Sweets," "Honey," or "Pal," was our second child and daughter, Támara. I began calling her "Roonie" due to the lip formation as a child, which tended to spit out Támar-ooon-a.

Flash 5

I have lived through the life and death of only one grand-parent, my Mimi—Edwidge Sauvé Girard. She died at age eighty-two, when I was not quite seven years old. I remember a loving, aged grandmother who loved to cuddle her "Bubúne." During her last year, however, her health began to fail. I wasn't able to chase her any longer. Nor was I able to smell the fragrant powder she patted daily on her face, the cosmetic custom of the day. I could no longer trace the history of my world with my finger tips. For a few months, she was put into a nursing home where I was allowed to stand under her window and, propped up, she would wave to my brother, Norman, and to me. I don't know whether she or I hated it more. She convinced her children that she needed to return home.

They all agreed and chipped in to provide home care. I was told that I had to be very quiet and not disturb her, especially when she was napping. It was all very confusing to me as a little boy living with someone who was no longer my same tactile and loving play partner.

I was allowed to go to her wake. I remember touching her now cold hand but was reassured that God had called her to a better place where she could be happy again. No one had much of an answer for me when I asked, "Why was it then that everyone is crying if Mimi was happy now?"

At her funeral—as was customary at the time—relatives were organized by age and placed in order of seniority by car, beginning with the oldest child of the deceased. Years later, my mother was still agonizing over the fact that she had inappropriately placed one of my uncles or aunts ahead of the other on the list. I was in the last direct-of-kin car in the procession with the other youngest grandchildren. My brother and next-of-kin cousins, all ten or more years older than me, proceeded to her burial in that car before more distant relatives and friends concluded the procession behind us. I remember asking what this was all about. I remember asking why people were crying. I remember asking where my mom and dad and Mimi were. There were no answers that I remember. My brother Norman, who always proudly protected me growing up, held my hand. But everyone was silent except for me; I had too many questions to ask.

I don't think that I realized the monumental event that was unfolding. I was the baby of the family. She was the only grandparent that I knew. My life as a small child was spent in her presence since she lived with us. Somehow, I didn't comprehend that life would be different without my Mimi. And I wasn't able to comprehend until much later in life how difficult the years after were for my mother who had lived for thirty-three years with her mother always under the same roof in one dependent form or another. I couldn't comprehend how my dad must have felt losing the second mother he loved so much. And I was incapable of realizing that my brother, who would have been her baby grandson for nearly seven years before my arrival on the scene, had now lost a significant part of his life as a young teenager.

During her life, our home buzzed with people frequently. Someone would come to visit, an elderly relative from Canada, an occasional granduncle or aunt, someone related whom she had raised. She was love incarnate to me and to the myriad of distant relatives who would come to visit. My parents' home was overflowing with near and distant relatives, especially during the holidays: her nine children, their spouses, their more than thirty children with their spouses and children, great-uncles and aunts, and distant cousins. When she died, my memories encompassed a significantly smaller number of relations. She was the matriarch. And I was the last of the clan. Judd reminded me of the moment, "For what are the words with which to summarize a lifetime, so much crowded confused happiness terminated by such stark slow-motion pain?"[3] She had lived a tough but beautiful life.

Even though I was only six years old, with my Mimi went a lifetime of my memories, to which nothing could ever be added. My life stopped with her for that instant, for those six plus years; and that early winter day that she died, I cast in stone a part of me that had died as well. She was singular in my life and in the lives of my brother and cousins. She was our very special treasure, never to be replaced. Through it all, I know that I have romanticized a small youth's infatuation with a woman larger than life, but she holds a most special part of her youngest grandson's heart to this day and always will. She was the singular contact with my ancestry whom I could touch and love. At the end of the day, she was my memory of a childhood long gone, yet a relationship that I will always cling to regardless of its accuracy or factuality in reality. She was my Mimi and I her "Bubúne." We were special to each other.

Families create memories. Hers and mine were a special—albeit short—moment in time that lives on as though the music has played on forever.

MARVIN JOSAITIS

Flash 6

As though they knew it and had planned it, my mother's brothers and sisters, who were all nine to twenty-five years older than she had begun to assume the role of surrogate grandparents, and they simply and naturally stepped into that role for the rest of my childhood. As the baby of her family, my mother was raised with three brothers and one sister old enough to be her parent. Many of them had children older than my mother. Some of them had grandchildren older than me. So they adapted easily and generously to a boy who might call them "Uncle" or "Aunt," but they functioned as much more. I can't recount the number of times that I would spend weekends or just the occasional day with them, having them spoil me, as grandparents usually want to do. For them, I was their baby sister's baby, and they stepped up to the task. I loved having them tell stories about my mother when she was growing up, or tales of my Mimi and her many relatives, and of a Pipi I never knew. Frequently, I would repeat the folklore to my mother who wondered where I had learned this or that; often she would put her own spin, allowing me to see that, over time, memories are imprecise in their embellishments. Her eyes would flutter when I would tell of being served breakfast in bed by my Aunt Marie or my Aunt Agnes, whom I called "Honey," or having a hot fudge sundae every time I visited. My mother quickly let me realize that these were special events not to be replicated at home.

Most important, our family continued to support each other after the death of our matriarch.

All of these family grandparent surrogates affected my life in values and direction. Uncle Arthur gave me the idea that I could become a musician like him. During the silent films, he played the fiddle during the intermissions and also played some of the background music required to enhance the silent screen. I decided in favor of the piano, and it was Uncle Arthur who eventually expanded my meager sheet music library with stacks of turn of and early twentieth-century music. Often, after playing it for the occasional "gig," frequently my audience will ask me the source of such melodious and spirited music.

Uncle Humphrey taught me a love for nature and animals and that we were all a part of nature, not apart from it. He was a kind family man who lived, as his parents had earlier in their life, on a farm. He loved his youngest sister dearly and engendered in me the importance of family "roots." After Mimi died, he organized the Girard family reunions, always trying to keep together families that have a tendency to drift apart after the parents die. His children—Vera, Marian, and Donald—and grandchildren keep the tradition going to this day.

Vera Freeman and Marian Bagwell taught me, with their beautiful, positive disposition and attitude toward living, to always view the world whether in suffering, pain, or happiness as a glass half full and never half empty. Aunt Agnes—Honey—was generous and caring despite difficulty in her marriage, but she taught me cheerfulness and a sense of lively spirit. Aunt Violet taught me to appreciate life's simple joys; she was a beautiful, unassuming, quiet, and humble person dedicated to her husband and three sons. And my other uncles, Alvin and Clifford, and my aunt Josie all had families pulling them in many directions; I simply spent less time with them. We all become victims of the exigencies that pull at us in different directions at varying times during our life. Each, nonetheless, contributed to my growing up as their youngest nephew.

Flash 7

My Aunt Marie and her husband, Uncle Tom, provided my dominant home away from home, enjoying free time with them as an *ersatz* "grandson" until they had grandchildren of their own to spoil and love. Their daughters, Lois and Norma, were like older sisters that I never had. They and their spouses—Harold (Hi) Harty, and John (Jack) Kearney—also reserved a special place for me in their young marriages and eventually introduced me as "Uncle Butch" at the end of my boyhood as they had had children of their own. As Judd has said, "For what are the words to summarize a lifetime?" They all simply were always there for me.

For me, Uncle Tom was the grandfather figure I never had, permitting me to sit on his lap while he captivated me with personal stories of life on a train as a caboose conductor. He even let me rub his shiny bald head during the tales. When I stayed with him overnight, in the morning he would lather my face along with his, hand me a bladeless razor, and teach me by example a ritual of manhood as we shaved together awaiting the special breakfast Aunt Marie was creating for her guys. I eventually replicated this with my own young children.

Twenty-three years ago, Norma and Lois asked me to deliver the eulogy at their dad's funeral—my Uncle Tom. As I stood at the pulpit and looked out beyond his casket, I saw at a glance the remains of and the growth of my Mimi and Pipi Girard's family. My mother, their youngest, was their only child still living. She sat surrounded by nephews and nieces, cousins, and my wife, Donna. In its sadness, it was also a celebration of several generations of an enduring, enriched family. Now there were more grandchildren and great-grandchildren carrying on the family, our family, with many different surnames, augmenting even further the Girards. In an instant, I experienced as a middle-aged man what incredible joy existed in making family. I took a deep breath and began the following eulogy:

> Thomas Edison and Henry Ford were young inventors, getting ready to make their contributions to society. The telephone had just begun to become available in urban areas. Talking pictures were still thirty years away. The flight of the first airplane at Kitty Hawk was still one year away. President McKinley had been assassinated and

Queen Victoria had ended her reign just one year earlier. Rough-Rider Teddy Roosevelt was in his first term as the twenty-sixth president of the United States, and the Victorian era of the nineteenth century had come to an end. The Spanish-American War had just ended. A new twentieth century had just dawned. It was Christmastime, 1902, and—in general—the world was at peace.

A baby was born during that peaceful era to James and Sarah Lewis O'Donovan in a little community called Pittston, Pennsylvania, on the banks of the Susquehanna River. They named him Thomas.

I need not convince anyone here today that life on the Susquehanna River in 1902 was not primitive, but neither was it luxurious. People growing up in that peaceful era scraped pretty hard for their living. Conveniences that we take for granted were yet to be discovered and experienced. The simplicity and less complex life patterns, nonetheless, provided a formula for success that many people of that era adopted.

Tom O'Donovan developed that formula and stuck to it throughout his life. While history was being written at astronomical rates of growth and activity in a faster-paced twentieth century, Tom O'Donovan was patiently writing his own history and making his own footprints in the sands of time. I hope you will permit me to suggest that his formula for a successful life was quite simple and basic. I intend this morning to outline that formula as best I can, piecing together from memory the characteristics that were, in my opinion, his hallmark.

Last night, after I was presented with the honor of delivering these reflections, I began to look through passages in Sacred Scripture, the writings of Kahlil Gibran and others for some inspiration. And then, I realized that I didn't have to go to any source other than Tom O'Donovan himself for this presentation. When you are privileged to know and love an exemplary person, there is no need to look for any other models. And Tom, my uncle, was indeed exemplary. So exemplary that as a two-week-old child, my parents selected Thomas as my baptismal name.

What my eyes and my memory can reproduce for you this morning is only half the story. Nearly half had been written by my uncle before I was even born. When I was born at Christmastime in 1941, he was already ending his fourth decade. But he seemed to change so little during my lifetime that I've concluded that the adult Tom O'Donovan we all knew was the same adult Tom O'Donovan who always was. For me, he symbolized the steady, the calming, the confident, the predictable during a very turbulent and changing period of time. His was the way of peace and quiet. If he was frustrated at times, I guess it may have been that—as adaptable as he was to a changing world and as much as he went along with the modern—he never could understand why the world hadn't discovered the simple formula to happiness and success that served him so well for so long. I think he felt that most people had made life far more complex, more stressful, and more confusing than it had to be. Perhaps he had learned from his Susquehanna

River days that you flow with a river and you don't buck the current if you want to live at peace with yourself and your world.

Permit me now to propose the formula that I think was his. I will use the six words that came to me last night when I reflected on the life of Tom O'Donovan. After I wrote down those words last night, I realized that the first letter of each actually spells THOMAS. As I walk through my memories, I hope that my thoughts will trigger similar thoughts of your own.

The first word was *train*. Tom worked for the New York Central Railroad as a conductor and brakeman for thirty-eight years. He loved to work, and he loved his work. He had every quality that employers hope to get in an employee. To begin with, he was a walking advertisement of the proud employee. To look at him always dressed up in his suit, white shirt, tie, Florsheim wingtips, this employee believed that every employee is really a president in his own right. He is the president of the job that only he can do day in and day out. Tom was proud that he was part of the transportation industry. He identified with it during a career at a time when railroads were as exciting as jet travel and rockets are today. He was faithful to his company and very saddened by the fates he didn't think railroads deserved. He nearly never missed a day's work. He sold his trade and was proud to be associated with it. As a small boy, I thought that my Uncle Tom was in the caboose of every train I saw. When I would wait at a crossing, I would ask my parents if he would wave to me—and despite what they said, I hoped that I would see him in that last car. To this day, whenever I wait for a train, I look for the caboose, and I remember him. I always look to see if the man inside might remind me of that beautiful memory. The first word *train*, then, points to the importance of taking pride in work that is so important to a fulfilling life.

The second word is *home*. One didn't really know Tom O'Donovan unless you realized how important his home was to him. He took pride in his house, whether it was in Detroit on Central Avenue or Mansfield Street or in Ann Arbor on Medford. And each house or apartment became his home. There he came, there he lived, there he entertained, there he raised his family, and, appropriately, there he died. He didn't see a real need to ever travel very far for very long away from his home. His home allowed him to find the peace and warmth and simplicity of lifestyle that he maintained. And most important, in addition to work, it defined who he was. And he was comfortable being that person. True to his simple upbringings, a home for him was not defined by prestigious address, unnecessary luxuries, and artificiality. His home was defined by the person he was and, at the same time, reflected back to the welcomed visitor the master of the home. The second part of his formula for happiness was: create a home environment in life where you love to be and where others love to visit.

The third word is *O'Donovan*. Tom never forgot his roots and the family in Pennsylvania, which was a part of those roots. He was always faithful to his family and to the family of his wife,

MARVIN JOSAITIS

my Aunt Marie. He had two families really—an O'Donovan family and a Girard family. Both were important to him. Both had his attention and involvement. The compassion and understanding and respect that he had developed in growing up with the first, he adapted to the other. Blood relatives and in-law relatives really meant the same to him. To this day, I have to make a special effort to distinguish him as an uncle through marriage from uncles by birth. I don't think it was an issue for him because the essential thing was that he had family—whether by adoption or birth, family for Tom O'Donovan was what really counted. And he raised his own daughters to feel the same. Add O'Donovan, meaning fidelity to roots and faithfulness to family, as the third formula for living as successfully as he did.

I have reflected on the *THO* of Thomas. These form the foundation stones for the final three, which define his formula more personally and emotionally.

The *M* word is *marriage*. Tom O'Donovan had a love affair with one woman for half a century. And, despite his acceptance of events that ended the physical relationship thirteen years ago, he continued that love affair in his own silent way. His Marie, he sometimes called Mary, particularly when he was in a teasing mood. No greater attestation of greatness can be given to any man, Lois and Norma, than to say that he loved your mother and was a faithful steward of their wedding vows. But it didn't stop there. Tom was blessed with two other beautiful women who were his pride and joy. Whenever I met Uncle Tom, he would always first ask me about my family and then, without even a prompt, he would immediately tell me about his daughters. To know Tom O'Donovan without knowing Lois and Norma was to know only a part of him. And through them, he acquired two sons: Harold and Jack. Again, they became his sons and he their dad.

In many ways, I was privileged to have an Uncle Tom who practiced being a grandfather on me. He would refer to his children as your Aunt Lois, your Aunt Norma, your Uncle Hi, and your Uncle Jack. This happened in our relationship until his own eight grandchildren and then nine great-grandchildren fulfilled his life while he was still alive. I was pleased and privileged to be the recipient of that grandfatherly love as a boy until his own were born. And nothing or no one in life defined Tom more than did all of his loves, the result of his first love, Marie. The personal commitments in *marriage* were a pre-eminent part of his formula for happiness.

The second last word is *associates*. Tom O'Donovan had friends and good friends all over the place. Maybe he invented the word *networking* before it became a vogue. Tom's friends could count on him, whether it was with a pat on the back, a conversation about solving the world's problems, a ten spot or more in time of need, sharing his good sense of humor, or just being together. And his friends he met in a variety of places: from his church to the neighborhood, from regular people on his walking route to waitresses at the end of the route, from a corner grocer to a friend at

MARVIN JOSAITIS

the racetrack, from a work associate in the railroad to a friend of a friend of a friend. People couldn't help but know he cared. And he was great company. His peaceful, gentlemanly, unassuming, undemanding personality was woven with a generous, loving, and fun-loving spirit. Grooming *associates* or friends was his fifth hallmark for success.

And finally, Thomas was a *sportsman*. This added the final balance to a fulfilled life. He wasn't athletic, but so what. He was comfortable in being himself. The three recreational loves of his life—and he did all of them exquisitely well—were walking, fishing, and horse racing. Too many men today lack hobbies or interests. Not Uncle Tom. I know of no one who for so long a lifetime was faithful to daily exercise. And he didn't just stroll—he really walked briskly. Growing up in a world without owning automobiles was not a disadvantage; he turned it into an advantage and stayed healthy. And sportsman he was in the truest sense of the word. I think that I first learned to fish with Uncle Tom at Sugarloaf Lake in Michigan. As a small boy, I would ask him why he threw back so many of the fish he caught. He taught me and others to love a sport for what it was and to respect life and nature for what it was. He was really an environmentalist and expressed his quest for peace this way as well. The same was true for thoroughbred horses. He loved the animals and their awesome beauty. He didn't have to place bets to enjoy his day. The power of nature and the discipline of the sport were his foremost interests at the track. His final message to me is the importance of *sportsmanship* and relaxation in life.

And those, my friends, are my reflections.

Through my eyes and heart—that was Thomas O'Donovan: your dad, your grandpa or great grandpa, your friend, my uncle. What a model of a man!

This Christmas will be the first in my lifetime that I have not had him to celebrate our end-of-December birthdays together. For years—wherever I lived in the United States of America, Canada, or Europe—the first birthday card to arrive in the mail was from him, without fail. I'll miss that tradition this Christmas, but I have so much to remember about him that is good and wonderful. And when I see the light on a caboose, I'll know that from his new world, he still is wishing me "Best wishes."

And, for those of you who will miss him in other ways, maybe if you remember the ideas of the French existentialist philosopher Gabriel Marcel, who lived approximately the same number of years as Uncle Tom, it will be a source of strength and peace. According to Marcel, to love someone means to say that for me, you will never die.

Lois and Norma, I hope that in some small way today, I have reinforced the reality that for you and us, your dad will never die. In your sadness, you must be more than proud that he is yours. I speak for everyone here when I say: Thank you for sharing your treasure with us for so long a time.

Looking over my family gathered there in Ann Arbor, Michigan, that day, I realized that, as baby of the Girard family, I had summarized the decades that had fulfilled the dreams of my immigrant grandparents, leaving their farm and carting their children across the Detroit River from Canada to a new world. Their dream lived on. The confusion that I had as a six-year-old burying the only grandparent I knew was now clarified and spoken and shared with my family. I realized that in the process I was also making family.

Flash 8

Throughout my early life, visiting my mother's family opened up my world and expanded my horizons unbelievably. I frequently had to take public transportation as a young boy to their homes, so a love of travel started at an early age. I sometimes wonder whether these visits to my surrogate grandparents gave me the wanderlust experienced as an adult when I moved our family to so many new homes. Perhaps this is where the gypsy in me first stirred.

Even the regular bus drivers on the routes that I would take learned my name. In fact, one of them—Mr. Morgan—would slow the bus as he approached our street; he would look down the street to see if I was doddling along and wait for me to run and catch his bus. I am sure that the passengers loved these delays! This same bus driver, years later, would do the same thing when I was a teenager taking several public buses to get to high school. Amazing if you think of it in today's world. And at the time, we lived in the nearest suburb south of metropolitan Detroit, at that time the fifth-largest city in the United States of America. Little wonder that my mother was comfortable when I turned ten with my taking the bus alone to downtown Detroit on a Saturday morning to spend the day window shopping and looking for future gift ideas. She would only say, "Don't go anywhere with a stranger." And she always asked if I had found any pennies on my travels.

Growing up in the '40s and early '50s, my mother was like most of her peers, the full-time homemaker. So her constant presence, augmented by my uncles, aunts, and eventually my closest married cousins inviting me over to spend time with them allowed me to realize that my family was ahead of Hillary Clinton's *It Takes a Village.*

And times in our neighborhood were different five to six decades ago than now. There were many neighbors who just happened to have cookies and milk waiting for me as I pounced into their kitchens for an occasional chat. I always told my mother where I was going, but if perchance I forgot, the neighbor would call to say where I was. All of them were addressed by "Mr." or "Mrs." except those who deserved a warmer "Uncle" or "Aunt" in front of their first names. Uncle Frank and Aunt Sally were two such people, childless, who adopted me in the neighborhood as their own. Until they died, their holiday card was always signed that way, even in my adult years. During the mid '50s, younger couples in the neighborhood preferred being called by their first names. This practice was difficult to adapt to, but times, "they were a' changing."

In those days, we had school buses but didn't have to use them. So for most of my youth, the mile walk to school was the time to explore the world. Open fields still existed then where homes are today. I would get muddy in the creek, catching crabs and frogs. There were the wild flowers to pick or even large dandelions, which in staining the hands of the picker brought a large smile as he handed them to his mother. What mother could get angry with a son's muddy shoes and clothes, receiving such gifts after a day in school and an equally adventuresome trip back home.

On my exploratory walks back and forth to school, I even befriended Mrs. Quandt who owned a farmette that I traversed. One May day, she interrupted my picking from her huge lilac bushes. She had scissors and appropriately cut a bouquet explaining that some older boys were damaging her bushes. She befriended me and said that, whenever I wanted a bouquet for my mother, each spring she would cut it for me if I asked. I never broke another branch and ended up having my own florist for five straight years. Even better, I didn't have to spend any of my allowance money. Of course, part of the deal was that I wouldn't tell our secret to any other kids! It takes a village.

PENNIES FROM A HEAV'N

Flash 9

My dad, Frank William Josaitis, was a gentle and kind man. His parents, a Lithuanian father, Franz (later called Frank), and a white Russian/Lithe mother, Ursula Zalenka, left Lithuania just after the dawn of the twentieth century with one daughter. They stopped in Germany to earn enough money to support their quest, living eventually with cousins in America. Their immigration from Europe was the story of so many grandparents of Americans my age. While in Germany, their first son and second child was born, followed by another son just after exiting Europe and entering the New World. By 1907, they were able to succeed in reaching Ellis Island where their name (probably Yesaides) was changed to the way the intake officer understood it.

Reaching Detroit, in time to be part of Henry Ford's auto revolution, my grandfather worked in maintenance at the Rouge for the now famous five dollars a day. Their fourth child and third son, my father, was born February 16, 1909. Their family was completed with a birth of another daughter prior to the start of World War I.

I wish that I had known my grandparents. Both died before the start of World War II, and I was born on December 27, 1941, twenty days after Pearl Harbor.

Whenever I visit Detroit, I try to drive by the house on the hill above Fort Street where they lived. Now, perhaps it isn't there anymore except in my memory. My grandparents lived hard lives but fulfilled their dreams before they reached what is considered retirement years. But each died at relatively young ages with dreams unfulfilled, leaving their children and eventually their grandchildren the heritage of an America where all could be possible.

My father left school at age sixteen to help my grandfather support not only his sister, but a very ill invalid mother whom he would carry in his arms moving her from room to room as she required. Undoubtedly, this dedication as a teenager was instrumental in chiseling him into the caring, domesticated man that he became. His older siblings were now adults out of the nest, living the typical lives of first generational immigrants of the time, forging new lives in a new country, trying not to give signs of the old world. My father, however, never forgot his roots and wasn't ashamed of parents who reflected another culture. (This same quality of his character occurred as a young married man, inviting his mother-in-law—herself an immigrant from Canada and a widow—to live with him and his new bride.) Fortunately, he was able to find work in a grocery store where he learned the meat-cutting trade. He worked as a meat-cutter for forty-six years, all but the first four of them with the Kroger Company.

From my dad, I had the pre-eminent example of a strong work ethic, honesty, and fidelity that is possible. During his life, I believe he missed one—maybe two—days of work. He had to be almost totally incapacitated before he would stay home. His mottos were simplistic truths like honesty is the best policy and never talk badly about someone else or misjudge another—unless, as the Dakota Sioux Indian prayer says, "you have walked in his moccasins for two weeks." If he had nothing good to say about someone, he would say nothing. Instead, in place of words, he would commence whistling a tune, pretending to be preoccupied. He was stoic, strong, and principled. At the same time, he was quiet and gentle.

Dad was faithful to friends. So faithful that, when his pheasant-hunting friend died an early and unexpected death, my dad felt that he couldn't hunt anymore: his friend couldn't hunt, so neither could he. Right or wrong, it was his sense of principled fidelity to a dear friend.

My mother was his special confidant throughout their nearly fifty years of marriage. My Mimi was his heroine and a second mother, and he loved having her live with us in our three-generation bungalow.

I grew up never questioning that a principled life was the only life worth living.

Perhaps one of my greatest kaleidoscope memories came as a young boy of five on a cold, early April evening in 1947. Henry Ford had just died. Henry Ford's company had provided employment for my grandfather. So my dad wanted my brother and me to be with him as he paid his respects to this giant of Detroit and American history, in his mind, the only person—other than FDR—who made life possible for his parents and himself. He held my twelve-year-old brother's hand and alternated holding mine with holding me in his arms so that the three of us in an interminably long line at the Dearborn Rotunda could pass by the bier of this industrial scion. I remember his telling me how important this man was to us. I've never forgotten the lesson of fidelity in this simple gesture of my father with his two sons.

Needless to say, my father was unbelievably proud when I took an assignment at Ford headquarters thirty years later. He would salute as he drove by the headquarters building, saying to himself, "My son works there." I am sure that he relived the days of his youth with an immigrant father who fulfilled his dreams not far from where his own son now worked. Whenever I had a chance, I would leave my office on the second floor of the Ford headquarters and find reason to visit the Dearborn Rouge Plant where my grandfather would have worked. For me, this was where the real Ford men were. I would do this at least once a month, and I would stop to talk with workers there, remembering a grandfather whom I never knew. Somehow, his spirit lived with me when I visited the Rouge.

MARVIN JOSAITIS

The most difficult discussion that I had with my father was the day that I decided to leave Ford Motor. My dad had worked forty-two years with one company. This was the way things should be for me as a custodian of fidelity to one's employer. My dad had a difficult time understanding that by the 1980s, domestic auto companies were undergoing great changes and companies in general had changed in their fidelity to their employees as well. It was now a different employment world. The workplace had changed and wouldn't have the same bond that existed between employer and employee during his work life. He listened to me, accepted my reasons, but I think he was disappointed. I think that the father holding his child at the bier of Henry Ford, proud of the fact that that son carried on the tradition of his own immigrant father, now had to adjust to a different type of loyalty than he had lived in his own life. The topic was never broached over the next three years while my dad was still alive. I think that he had been wounded in some way by my decision, even though he always respected the paths that I eventually took.

My brother and I grew up with a father who constantly reminded us that each of us could become and be anything that we wanted in life with hard work and perseverance. The only thing he excluded was our becoming meat cutters. Hence, he always performed this role at home and wouldn't teach us his skills. Needless to say, he was extremely supportive of higher education for his sons and was enormously proud that a high school dropout and a high school diploma spouse would parent two men who eventually earned doctorates. In my own mind, his dedication to family, work, and principled living earned him an honorary degree.

In 2003, twenty years after his death, my son Tarik and his wife, Archana, sent me a Hallmark Father's Day card with the picture of a young boy learning to ride a bicycle for the first time and a father's gentle hand steadying his back. The words of the card were words that I often use in kaleidoscopic remembrances of my dad: "You encouraged me, you supported me, you guided me. You always told me I could grow up to be anything I wanted … and one thing I grew up to be was very thankful for having a father like you."

My father's family needs as a sixteen-year-old, his own wife and children, and later his only three grandchildren were his raison d'être. He died six weeks shy of celebrating his fiftieth wedding anniversary with my mother. He was, in short, a family man par excellence.

The third son of an immigrant father, Dad watched with pride his own two sons grow and develop lives that appeared would be childless. Both of his sons became Catholic priests, apparently bringing to an end his lineage. He supported these decisions of ours. However, after I resigned the clergy[4] and then married, he also used the birth of our first child, Kateri, as his excuse to retire so that he and my mother would have time to spend with their granddaughter. And, time they did.

My parents lavished attention and presence, not material things, on Kateri for the three years during which she was their only grandchild. As each new grandchild entered their lives, they produced more and more love

MARVIN JOSAITIS

enkindled with rich memories. By the time their third and final arrived, their lives were complete. After all, each of my parents had dedicated themselves to their family of two sons, which now had grown with the additions of a daughter-in-law, two granddaughters, and one grandson. The latter four they had never expected. For my mother, these were truly pennies from a heav'n. For my father, they were maybe even better than copper.

Flash 10

Growing up with Frank and Margaret Josaitis was a gift that neither my brother, Norman, nor I had done anything to deserve. The love and attention that they showered on us daily was only surpassed by the love and attention they continually demonstrated for each other. The two of them had given themselves to each other on July 3, 1934, and their love vows lasted a lifetime together. They were really a romantic couple in an unassuming, quiet way, much like the characters in Virginia Woolf's deservedly acclaimed *To the Lighthouse*. Whether spoken or not, whether expressed in words or not, to live under the same roof with my mom and dad was to know that a stream-of-consciousness love affair was constantly in the making.

During my upper high school years, my fascination with Virginia Woolf's novels mysteriously brought me back to the Frank and Margaret I watched carefully as my models and heroes in life. Moments would emerge when they would simply be looking at each other or sitting in the same room and their countenance quietly shouted that we live a wonderful life together. Disagreements and voiced anger were rare, but when they emerged, the salve of love endured. What eventually transpired brought anew a beautiful sunrise or sunset to move on beyond the insignificance of the moment, given the exigencies of the lifetime ahead. Norman and I realize today that we hadn't deserved their wonderful gifts of simple and genuine humanity carved into the beautiful, unassuming parents that they were.

Maybe the times also helped. The 1940s with the war, the rationing, the concern for one's fellowman whether here or abroad, the simplified lifestyles—all of these perhaps helped to focus on what is really important in life. And the post-war years of the early '50s continued the movement for national recovery with everyone chipping in. I guess at the end that our more complex, highly technological, fast-paced lifestyle today clouds the value of the times to which I refer.

During our formative dependent years of life, my parents spent time with their two sons. We listened to the radio shows together and laughed and discussed what was being said. We went to movies together. We prepared food together. We were a unit whose very existence depended upon constant attention to one another's well being.

I never remember being with a hired babysitter. After my Mimi, who lived with us died, whenever my parents visited friends or relatives, my brother and I went with them. If we got tired, we simply crawled up on a nearby couch and waited for the welcoming call, "It's time to go home." And their friends or relatives became part of the village family that was raising us to be the future men, the standard-bearers for society. Consequently, we were included in everything "real" transpiring around us: the problems occurring in lives around us, the events in other people's lives, the good and the bad, the joys and sorrows, and—ultimately—death. Nothing was kept from us. We were expected to be a part of and involved in life's joys and life's vicissitudes. This was Gail Sheehy's *Passages* being experienced and lived at every turn. Mom and Dad did not shelter us from reality. And they didn't shelter us from their interpretations of what growing up and living meant.

In addition to going to church together, we had our daily and weekly rituals.

Going to school was our workday. No excuses, no absences unless through sickness, and keeping noses to the grindstone. Our parents supported and reinforced the teachers, even if we complained or moaned; they knew the value of maintaining discipline and authority inside and outside the home. We quickly learned that, had we acted inappropriately during the school day, we would be heard—but Mom and Dad would never create a conflict with due authority. They would express openly their concern about our feelings, but would also express their disappointment that we had not acted appropriately to those who carried on their responsibility as parents under a different role: teacher. Disappointing behavior with teachers reflected back to them as disappointing behavior with parents. And so, Mom and Dad reinforced responsible authority in our lives.

Food rituals also occurred. Since Dad worked late on Fridays, our job was to help Mom make the Lithuanian version of potato pancakes, a recipe that Norman and I cherish to this day, albeit a time-consuming task that it was and is. Potato pancakes á la Lith, complete with the prepared mustard sauce rather than sour cream, comprised the Friday evening meal that we would proudly have ready when Dad returned from work. We always made enough so that there were leftovers for Saturday morning breakfast or even lunch. Early in life we had learned that too few pancakes meant arguments between brothers. So plenty were grated and cooked to be available for two growing boys the next morning or early afternoon. Saturday night, Dad always cooked the hamburgers. Sunday morning, we all worked together on frying the bacon and cooking the eggs in its grease. Sunday afternoon, we helped prepare the roast beef or smoked ham with all the trimmings. The food ritual was part of making family.

Thinking back fifty-sixty years, our family life combined play and work. Norman and I had assignments that justified an allowance, which we could use to purchase the "non-essentials." Our parents were meticulous do-it-yourselfers and taught us the proper way of maintaining a lawn, landscaping, and gardening. Inside the home, we learned how to paint, wallpaper, repair, and use tools.

Projects were accomplished together. Our home, in actuality, formed a microcosm of life: work, play, shelter, support, and love.

At the heart of this family were Frank and Margaret (Girard) Josaitis. Their lives were exemplary, but not easy. They had continued a dynasty of their immigrant parents. They had continued their dreams of a wonderful life in urban Detroit and eventually suburban Lincoln Park. Their two sons, Norman and Marvin, for them represented their contribution to the making of family in twentieth-century America. They, in their fading years, never ceased to support their sons. And today, at least one of them continues to surprise the wise onlookers with pennies from a heav'n.

Flash 11

Mom and Dad loved to travel. One might accurately label them adventuresome people. Throughout their marriage, they traveled generally by car. In anticipation of my father's vacation every summer, we would have a family caucus to determine what new worlds our family would discover by auto tour. This had begun when their family consisted of just my brother and Mimi. The four of them would go someplace together every summer. And when Bubúne arrived, things didn't change. I still remember Norman telling me about my first trip to Florida during the summer of '42. On that trip, I was transported in a baby basket wedged between him and Mimi, my traveling protectors and playmates. The safety car seats now commonplace didn't exist then.

Dad always drove, and Mom tended to the maps. In fact, my mother didn't get her driving license until I was out of college. During the car trips, she also entertained us and taught us to play car games—probably to minimize the "Are we there yet?" questions. Sometimes for hours we would be watching from our respective windows seeing who would be the first to spot whatever. And we each had a chance to create different car games. I would also whittle away the time standing behind her combing her hair, a practice that clearly would be viewed as unsafe today. But it worked then. As my hands combed and teased her thick, dark-brown wavy hair, she undoubtedly was remembering the not-too-distant past when her own mother had "Bubune," the young hair-dresser, performing in similar fashion.

Because Dad eschewed super highway driving as a poor way to really see things, when we could, we generally took alternate routes. These roads meandered through small towns and villages—places that allowed us to stop and absorb local flavors, cultures, and customs. The clock did not guide us because this was a vacation; whether we arrived at a particular destination didn't so much matter as how we arrived and what we experienced in the process. And during the meals we would talk about the places we saw or experienced that day. Our lunches were roadside picnics, which also permitted growing boys time to expend some energy after a morning of sitting. As evening approached, we began searching for a cabin or a motel, and this became a game as well since we all voted on which one looked right for that night.

MARVIN JOSAITIS

Traveling with "Explorer" Frank and "Guide" Margaret encouraged and developed a vagabond, almost gypsy spirit in us. This probably explains why Norman and I both love traveling and experiencing new cultures. It probably also translated into my excitement as well as easy adaptability with moving to different jobs, changing careers, and relocating my spouse and children to three different countries. My wife, Donna, sighs that this phenomenon probably contributed greatly to my penchant for moving to different homes, now up to sixteen in our forty-one years of marriage with seven years in our current home being the maximum.

Dad loved the mountains and the rural. Working and living in the Detroit area, his idea of a vacation did not include visiting major cities. Cities with specific and unique historic charms were the exception. Nonetheless, wherever our car managed to take us, the driver accommodated the needs of his wife, who wanted to at least stop and browse through a Stuckey's food shop or a gift shop along the way. This added to the variety and local color experiences.

So mountains and rural it was. The Smoky Mountains with side trips to every scenic pull-off, monument, or vista also provided favorite haunts in Gatlinburg and Cherokee. Along the way, caverns or waterfalls beckoned the four of us. Michigan's two peninsulas and Mackinac Island provided several years of trips around the Great Lakes. Included were side trips to Michigan's bordering states and province. The Gaspé peninsula in Quebec along with Quebec City (an exception to the no-city rule due to its unique charm) leading into the Canadian Maritimes and eventually New England created other unique explorations. Whether it was the French Quarter in New Orleans, the Mississippi River's historical towns and southern plantations, historical Williamsburg, the complete Skyline drive from its northern tip to its last southern exit, wanderlust in the summer beckoned us as a family. And we loved it.

Dad did all the driving. Consequently, with only one driver, exploring east of the Mississippi from a Michigan base became more practical. But each son had the thrill of eventually contributing to the tour at the wheel when we reached the magical driving age. This transition continued even into adulthood where other parts of the continent were explored together, they with either Norman or me. Greater distances became easier to accomplish with two qualified drivers. And so the western states beckoned and became the new haunts for the mountain lovers. My father loved reading novels, especially about the Old West, with Zane Grey's being his absolute favorites. Consequently, these western trips took on an even more special meaning for him.

Summer travel adventures created fodder for yearlong family discussions—but more—they created memories, family memories to cherish. And, at the end, we are left with the memories.

MARVIN JOSAITIS

Flash 12

If our family's auto tours provided the pièce de résistance of the summer, Big Portage Lake became our very own magic kingdom and frontier land for the remainder of each summer—long before Disney marketed the concept. A spring-fed, 680-acre, downstream repository to a chain of lakes connected by the Huron River, Big Portage Lake bridges Livingston and Washtenaw Counties thirty miles west of Ann Arbor, Michigan, in the Waterloo Recreation Area. Big Portage is nestled below Peach Mountain en route from the small town of Dexter to the even smaller town of Pinckney.

Somewhere in the early 1940s, my father befriended Hubert and Hilda Luke, middle-aged customers in his meat-cutting department at the Kroger Store in Dearborn.

Hubert, a Brit by birth, and Hilda, a Finn, were a childless couple who both served people through the medical profession—he, as a patient intake officer/counselor at a nearby sanitarium and she, as a licensed practical nurse for a group of physicians.

The Lukes had just purchased their vacation retreat, a peaceful solace perched above a wooded ravine at Fox Pointe, at the time the last cottage development on the southeastern shore of Big Portage Lake. The Lukes loved their hideaway but at the same time felt deeply that their treasure hideaway should be shared with their friends and few distant relatives. How fortunate the day that they asked their new friend, Frank Josaitis, to visit them with his wife and his two sons! That day, a magical love affair began between two boys and a lake, an affair that actively lasted for more than a quarter of a century, an affair that continues today through the kaleidoscope of memories.

At first sight from the outside, the cottage was not a candidate for *Better Homes and Gardens*. In its original form, it would be called a handyman's delight in any real estate advertisement today. The two rooms, the Luke's bedroom, large enough for a double bed and one dresser, and a combination kitchen/eating/meeting room with exposed beams and linoleum floors were complemented by a screened back porch, which faced the ravine leading to the lake. The latter was fitted with two double beds separated by a curtain for privacy; storm windows hinged to the slanted roof beams could be lowered during rainy weather. The cottage was not insulated appropriately for winter use. But the chipmunks that hid in the crawlspace and played hockey with acorns on the roof didn't mind, and neither did we.

An actual pre-refrigerator, non-electric icebox, a small electric stove, and a pot-bellied wood stove were the appliances and HVAC systems. A carport with a shed for storage protected the front of the house. Eighty feet to the right of the front door, a one-seater outhouse sat privately behind a cluster of pines and cedars. A non-electric hand water pump graced the path midway down the ravine where the daily routine of carrying buckets of water from the well to the main room of the house for the needs of the day made the cottage a truly special place. Like true boy scouts, Norman and I would vie for the honors and, to our surprise, no one seemed to compete with us.

Throughout the '40s, as the Lukes' savings increased sufficiently, with the physical help of their friends, changes occurred. Luke puttered as an ersatz carpenter and handy man and welcomed any skill that others could offer. After all, this was not designer-ville. A professional interior decorator or skilled carpenter would have shuddered with the practical building creations of this unlikely team of builders. What truly excelled as important was that their friends would continue to be comfortable sharing this oasis with them. It would not become the house that Luke built but rather the home away from home that had meaning for every contributor within their village of friends. Luke knew enough psychology to make one wonder now whether he bonded his friends intentionally and cleverly through these group endeavors. Planned or not, it worked. The Lukes had discovered before Antoine de

Saint-Exupéry's *Little Prince* did that "what is essential is invisible to the eye."

Hilda and Luke kept a calendar to mark down when so-and-so or so-and-so would be planning to visit. Depression, for them, was defined as being at their lake home with no one sharing it with them. And so their closest friends all knew where the key was hidden. Luke and Hilda even rejoiced when they could arrive to a cottage on a Friday evening already bubbling with life. They expected that our family would spend at least two weeks plus any weekends when others weren't with them from late spring until mid-autumn. Additionally, they would telephone to let us know when the calendar was empty, expecting and hoping that we would accommodate the vacancy. And we usually did. Sometimes, they would pick up Norman and me on a Friday evening when our parents only could come later that weekend.

By the turn of the decade, the ice-box graduated to relic status as a memorable cupboard and a used electric refrigerator with a small freezer big enough to hold ice cream and ice cubes now graced a kitchen that had running water at the sink and an electric heating furnace near the interior wall. The carport eventually was glass-enclosed in order to function as a living room during the day and a bedroom at night, thanks to the pull out couches making this possible; what a practical solution to assure Luke and Hilda that even more of their friends could be together at the cottage. And, by the early '50s, the attached shed progressed from storage to a combination toilet and laundry room complete with a stand-alone shower stall.

The dining part of the kitchen/gathering room always retained the same character: a picnic table with checkered oilcloth and benches and a pole light chandelier. The table functioned as Luke's desk whenever meals were finished. There he read newspaper, novels, and more meaty professional journals prolifically—well beyond others' bedtime. When he vacated this spot, he either napped or did some minor handyman chore. When the pole light dimmed, we all knew that Luke had finally retired. And, of course, he loved to discuss major issues of the day around that "board room table," solving them in council with his friends. Hilda tidied the home regularly and afterwards sank in her rocker, chatting with whomever wanted to watch the world turn. Frequent discussions revolved around the current events occurring in the lives of all the friends present or absent. We re-lived the village. After all, what mattered more than the people who had become the heart of their cottage?

A few unwritten rules of the cottage were known almost by osmosis, the primarily one: having fun among friends. Consequently, anger or arguments had no place in the Portage magic kingdom. The second rule: bring your own food and drinks; no other monetary fee existed for guests at the "inn." Whenever this was violated, Hilda and Luke would quickly go, without expressing their disappointment, to the country store to make sure that their undeserving guests would be fed. My parents and other generous friends often chipped in to help the Lukes with guests who conveniently forgot to provide for themselves. When this happened, however, rule one still carried the day. Rule three: the evening meal would have a place setting in case an unexpected friend arrived. The fourth rule was that everyone prepared food, relieving Hilda from becoming a slave to her hospitality—except for Sunday dinner. By choice, Hilda always prepared the chicken before we returned to the city. Fried chicken á la Hilda, complete with dumplings and gravy was ritualized for decades. To this day, try though I may, I still cannot replicate this gourmet meal. And unwritten rule five: one bedroom in the house was never used, except by the inn-keepers. The smallest room of the house was revered as Hilda and Luke's space, out of deep respect for the generous couple who orchestrated their own version of the 1940s film *The Enchanted Cottage*.

The Lukes were technically a childless couple. However, one winter in the early '40s they adopted Ginger, a dark-grey, slightly speckled, male English bull terrier pup. By summer, they introduced the newest member of the family to us, his cute, wrinkled pug face gleaming with pride and pleasure. The Lukes put the time and energy that other couples did with their progeny into Ginger. In one breath, Ginger was adorable, cute, spoiled, precocious, faithful, friendly, playful, singular, unique, charming, lovable, protective, involved—just what anyone could hope for in man's best companion. He knew not only how to please Hilda, Luke, and all their friends but how to easily become part of the family. So well trained, we needed to spell certain words, like "leash," "home," "Luke's coming" because Ginger would go berserk with excitement if he heard the spoken word.

Ginger loved being one of the guys and sidled up to the Josaitis boys for as much attention, play, and involvement that we were willing to give. This included everything from playing Frisbee to swimming in the lake to accompanying us in our frequent rowboat excursions. Ginger grew up with us, arrived first to adulthood, and became a senior citizen in the late '50s before Norman and I left our youth behind. Strange how three "boys" who spent summers together could take such different paths.

Unexpectedly, one late autumn day, when I returned from high school, my mother informed me that the Lukes were planning a quiet weekend at the cottage amidst the falling leaves, all alone for a change. By their unusual request, they asked their friends to allow them time to be alone. They had just buried our playmate and their "child" at his and our favorite haunt. I cried then, as I still do, thinking about those beautiful times together. Years later, as Hilda sat in her rocker to discuss friends and relatives with us, we would reminisce about the antics and spirit of Ginger. After a while, Hilda would get up quietly from her rocker to get her favorite drink, a Pepsi. This was our signal that the conversation should change to different memories when she returned.

The cottage was the heart of the Portage kingdom for us—a strong, thriving, pulsating, regular, beating heart—providing ongoing life for Luke and Hilda's chosen ones. But the soul of the experience, day in and day out, year in and year out, was the "Lake" itself. We went to "the Lake." It defined who we became.

What can one say in a few select words to describe more than a place where you have shared your youth? The Lake and its splashing, living waters became teacher, friend, companion, playmate, refuge, and mystery. Around its undeveloped shores, we picked wild raspberries in July. From the lagoon where Luke kept his rowboat, we would row into the pear-shaped lake itself and explore worlds beyond our imagination. The lake was our frontier land as we rowed across its waves to what we called Mud Bay, an undeveloped inlet inhabited by thousands of croaking frogs and large mud turtles sunning away the day, blinking at us as we drifted by their lily pad chaise lounges. We discovered Mud Bay in its isolation as the pre-eminent fishing hole, the place where fish spawned and beckoned two young boys to toss in a line with bobber.

The icebox needed replenishing with food and ice during the week when Dad or Luke had driven their cars into the city to work. But the lake beckoned. Into the rowboat climbed Hilda, dressed in a summer silk, Ginger perched at the bow, and Mom, comfortable in shorts—all awaiting the willing slave oarsmen who would transport this royal entourage to the country store, located at the southwestern part of the lake. There we would shop for the needed supplies, not least of which were night crawlers for fishing, snacks for Ginger, and a block of ice for our "box." During the really hot days of July and August, a full week or two at the Lake, meant several trips for the oarsmen, since the sun enjoyed half melting the ice, turning its block into a sliver of its former self. Back and forth we would merrily row, making sure that our nourishments had refrigeration.

Marvin Josaitis

Our adventure land encompassed more than Big Portage Lake. Eventually, Norman and I were old enough and strong enough to spend the whole day, weaving and paddling by canoe through the chain of lakes. Little Portage Lake, one-eighth the size of its consort, provided the warm up for our journey. From there we headed north, paddling into the Huron River and, while dodging hidden rocks in its shallower areas, watched for the almost hidden entrances to Baseline Lake. Then it was up stream to Gallagher Lake, Strawberry Lake, Tamarack Lake, Whitewood Lake, and Zukey Lake before we would turn around to retrace our water path back to the largest lake of the chain, our lake. Each lake had its own special character and intrigue, but none, for us, could compare to "Portage."

Canoe trips became those special events, made even more special because we would laugh at the times that Luke attempted to forage our discovery via his boat with motor. Our job was to sit on either end of the boat, watching for the hidden rocks, which in their hunger, munched on "props." Norman or I would shout to Luke as one approached, allowing him to sway, twist, and dodge the protrusion inches under the surface awaiting the taste of a new morsel from his Mercury motor. Unfortunately, we were not always successful. Luke carried a few spares to repair his injured engine. After a couple of failed ventures, Hilda gently chastised Luke and suggested that he stop acting as one of the boys, only to spend his day in frustration with just a sunburn on his fair Englishman's skin to show for his efforts. We returned to our canoes without Luke.

It was the Lake where Dad taught us to swim, Norman better than I, and to dive off of the raft. It was the Lake that laughed with us as we cascaded into its welcoming arms at the end of the journey down the twelve-foot slide. It was the Lake that taught us the art of searching for shells along its shore and the architectural craftsmanship of building sand castles on its soft beach. It was the Lake, which allowed us to bathe and relax in its rich moisture and lie at its side as we slept with this aquaria lover under the summer's sun. It was the Lake that showed us the sport of speed boating with Luke as he attached the Mercury engine, changing a rowboat into a new adventure. It was the Lake that allowed us to view the beauty of sailboat races, which began the summer season in all their glory at the yacht club on its northwest shore. It was the Lake that taught us the simple beauty of nature as two young fishermen, accompanied by parents, watched from the boat the morning mist slowly lift eerily across its glassy stillness in a hallelujah chorus to the rising sun. It was the Lake that asked us to sit at its shore every evening and watch the sunset, dressing its azure tones with brilliant splashes of reds and golds, mixed with magentas and slowly changing colors of the spectra. It was the Lake that reflected in its waters the borealis spectacle shimmering above like the sparkling eyes of a diva in a summer play. This splendorous August night made it impossible to determine where the sky began and the water ended. It was the Lake where two boys learned to live under the tutelage of a wise teacher and dream dreams of worlds to come. It was the Lake. Always for us, it was the Lake. For

MARVIN JOSAITIS

Norman and me, it will always be the Lake that helped define who we were and who we became.

Rain or shine, the Lake fulfilled the unspoken rule *numero uno*: always have fun. I've just described the fun that the Lake provided for its favorite customers whose parents had to remind them daily that it was time for lunch or a break from the sun's rays. But neither did rainy days inside the cottage disappoint energetic lads. We would play cards or Chinese checkers for hours with our parents, the Lukes, or other friends. For variety, we would intersperse our gaming with reading, cross word puzzles, or listening to stories from our down-to-earth hosts about England or Finland or their recent excursions to the deserts of Arizona. The latter had beckoned them to winter there after they reached their retirement years. Once TV arrived, it altered the pattern very little.

Our favorite indoor pastime during these so-called inclement days was having the small, wiry amateur magician Luke entertain us with his latest magical trick, using either a deck of cards or the mysterious art of wizardry from beneath the black veil. He even had a white-tipped, black magic wand, a cape, and a top hat. After a round of thunderous clapping and laughing, should the sun replace clouds and raindrops, back to the lake we would go, but not before playing a game of horseshoes in the sand pits that Luke conveniently built next to the cottage. All the adults and kids had team tournaments at the pits that created wonderful rivalries and excitement as metal clanged against metal and the shoes either leaned against the post, encircled it, or flew out pointless. Each in their own ways, the Lake and the cottage never failed in fulfilling the role of magic kingdom and frontier land.

By the mid-60s, my mother phoned to tell me that Hilda would be returning from Arizona, where she and Luke had wintered after they retired, to the cottage that summer—without Luke. She didn't need to elaborate. I knew in her carefully selected words that it was time for me to cry again, as I had when I learned about Ginger. But the loss this time was beyond words. It still is. I had never adequately thanked Luke for all that he meant to me. I think he knew. I hope so.

In 1969, I began dating Donna Marie Rimer. That summer I introduced her to the cottage, to the lake, and to our own "Lady of the Lake," now an eighty-year-old. The years had kept her basically the same smiling lady who resembled, in reality, Cinderella's animated fairy godmother. She dressed the same as my Mimi had in a comfortable housedress, only her thicker reading glasses and hair now totally white gave away her aging secrets. Hilda loved Donna immediately and welcomed her as yet another part of the village of friends. That summer we explored with what little time we had some of my boyhood haunts. She began to see me through the eyes of Big Portage Lake and its environs. We climbed trees together, played at the beach, swam in the luscious, comforting waters, and sat watching the sunset and dreaming our dreams as the borealis of August skies danced in reflection on the still waters.

The following summer, Hilda welcomed Donna's parents and her brother as new guests to the clan. They had a

MARVIN JOSAITIS

chance to chat with her as she rocked and a chance to enjoy the Sunday afternoon chicken ritual before returning to the city. The next summer, we handed our firstborn to Hilda, who cradled our five-month-old Kateri as she sat in her rocker. Hilda told me that it didn't seem that long ago that she and Luke had held a special baby in their arms when Frank and Margaret first introduced their sons to them. We talked about those days. I made sure that Hilda heard me thank her for all that she and Luke, the cottage, and the Lake meant to me. And then, quietly, Hilda rose from her rocker, handed Donna and me our baby, walked into the kitchen, and returned with her favorite drink, a Pepsi. We knew that it was time to change topics.

The Lake called us to return with our toddler so that she could be introduced to its charms as a young boy had been nearly three decades earlier. My kaleidoscope can still focus clearly on a toddler running up and down the beach sometimes with and sometimes without a bathing suit, caressing the soft sand, carrying a bucket back and forth to a whispering lake who was entranced with watching a little girl build her first sand castles on its shore. Families create memories, and some of them are enhanced by a part of nature that can take on its own élan. This was and is the wonder and the mystery of the lake, which had helped raise me. It ended there, with a toddler too young to dream dreams, except through the two most important people in her young life who sat at the shore of the lake and did it for her.

Just before the summer of 1973, we learned that Hilda would not be going to the lake again. My mother didn't need to elaborate. Our own magic kingdom was now assigned a most special place in the hearts of its most frequent visitors. Hilda had three great loves throughout her life: Luke, Ginger, and Portage Lake. She had mourned the loss of her husband and special pup years before with the help of the Lake always there to comfort her, soothe her, and remind her of rich memories from the wonderful past spent at its shores. Now, as fate would have it, it was the Lake's turn to mourn and learn to cope without the presence of Hilda, who along with her two loves had graced its shores all those years from their enchanted cottage on the hill. The Lake had now lost its beloved and ever-faithful soul mate.

MARVIN JOSAITIS

Flash 13

How often I hear people my age (sixty-nine) reminisce about the part of their lives they loved the most, the period when they were raising their children. When I retired from corporate life in the late '90s to do other things and work that impassioned me, I had asked our three children to write down what each remembered about growing up in the Josaitis household. Their flashes that follow are the memories they chose to transcribe in a gift to me on Father's Day, 1999: "You have given us so much over the years," they wrote, at last we present you with reflections from our childhood. Dad, thank you for all of our memories. As you can tell from the pages that follow, we had a happy and safe childhood, filled with numerous experiences that have helped shape us to become who we are today. You have been a role model, friend, and teacher. Wow! Could I ever ask for more from my three munch-kins: Kateri, Támara, and Tarik?

Marvin Josaitis

Flash 14

Kateri, our first child, born January 20, 1971, dictated the following letter to me as I watched her through the nursery glass at Seaway Hospital in Trenton, Michigan, a special place where all three of our children would enter into our lives. Kateri is an Iroquois name meaning, "Flower of the Red Man." An Indian maiden named Kateri was also a "Lily of the Mohawks." Three days after her birth, Kateri asked me to hand deliver her dictated letter to her mommy:

> Dear Mommy,
>
> Since I'm already three days old, I thought it about time we have some "girl talk"—just between you and me. I want to thank you for holding me so close to your heart again. I was afraid you'd let me on my own too much after being one flesh for nine

months. I think you're really swell to me. When the nurse brings me back to the nursery, I say: Wow! That was really something having mommy feed me, cuddle me, and talk so sweetly to me. Imagine that! Wow! I'm sorry if I don't always do exactly as I'm supposed to, but maybe I'll learn … just got to hope you're patient with my growing up. Let me tell you I really do feel like a princess when I'm with you. And then, when I get back with the gang I feel like I'm the luckiest girl—for that matter the luckiest baby—in the whole nursery. Some of the other kids say, "Boy, Kateri, is that your mommy? She's really something else!" One boy even tried whistling at you the other day, but you didn't hear him cuz of the window in our nursery. That made me proud, too.

Since we're having our girls' chat, I'll tell you a secret if you promise not to tell anyone else. Do you cross your heart and promise? Well, the other day, Daddy was talking to me through the window—I heard him, but I pretended I was sleeping. He said, "Kateri, it wasn't too long ago that I was lonely and in need of someone very special. And your mommy brought the most happiness any man would ever want into his life with her tenderness, sensitivity, charm, beauty, warmth, and love. It was through your mother that I began to become someone. She is my special love. But I never dreamed that she would bring another woman so quickly into my life. Now I have two women, one very very special and one waiting to capture a different but also special place—the latter is you, Kateri. Right now as I look at you, you look externally ready to become as pretty as your mom ... that will just come naturally. My real hope is that you will be able to become even one half the lady, woman, girl, and lover your mother is, because someday there will be another man who needs someone just like I do. Fortunately, I have my bride already—and we'll try to prepare you for someone else, so that someday he'll be standing where I am talking to his little girl or boy about you. Sleep tight, my Sweet; I must go to my bride and be near her because without her I have no song for you."

That's my secret, Mommy. All I can say is wow; you're really someone special.

Love,

Kateri xxxooo

Flash 15

After forty years of making marriage and of becoming one with each other anew every day, I still feel the same about Kateri's mommy and am thankful every day that we still share and build our lives together as one. She is the shining star on the hill that our children and grandchildren look up to in wonder, thanking me that I have shared her and continue to share her unselfishly with each of them.

Years ago, when we would go out on our special "dates," to get away from the kids for a bit, I would write on a paper napkin in the restaurant and pass it over to Donna when she returned from a powder break. On the outside of the napkin, I would write: "MAJOR TRUTH." On the Inside: "I LOVE YOU." Donna still has one of those ink-faded napkins, an attestation that through it all, our love endures and grows.

Flash 16

Twenty-eight years later, Kateri wrote her own contribution to my kaleidoscope of memories on Father's Day, 1999:

Pops,

You have always been there for all of us with love, tenderness, and compassion. As far as I am concerned, and in whatever lifetime, you will always be! You always made me feel special and always loved! Some comfort memories from early on cause me often to reflect back and smile. I remember the special bedtime songs when you would sing: "I love you a bushel and a peck, a bushel and a peck and a hug around the neck, a hug around the neck and a barrel and a heap..." or the one you created: "Lollipops and popsicles, lollipops and popsicles, lollipops and popsicles melt the summer away and we have so much fun, and we do so many things, like laughing and singing and jumping and whatever 'ing' action that came to mind…"

I remember squealing: "One more time, Pops," or putting a finger aside my nose as a small girl and whispering, "Time."

I do remember when I was the only child; maybe some pictures helped out, too. But when my sister, Támara, came along at age three, I was so excited. You and Mom made sure that I was an important person in this event! I remember getting to sit in the little green rocking chair to be the first one to hold her! There was no feeling of jealousy or having to share "my mom and dad" because I was the "big sister." I just remember feeling really important. All smiles! Then when Tarik came along and I was five, both Támara and I got to "share" the first hold to welcome our little brother, once again feeling like an important person. This entire first welcoming step, albeit a small thing, is probably why the three of us are the way we are today. We were never jealous siblings; although we were big on "fairness," because we knew that we were all equals and important people in each other's lives, just like the first time we all met in a welcoming lap embrace.

Támara and I would bug Dad about doing "boy" things with our brother, who would taunt us by saying: "Only the boys." So you decided to join Indian Princesses with us, special times that we had only with our dad: crafts, food, camping, horseback riding, weekends away...just with you. You were called "Two Fawns in our tribe, but we felt brave calling you "Bald Eagle." I think that illustrates the "special" relationship we had. Our dad was always a "teaser," so why not tease back and have fun. And we did. Not many dads would have gone to Indian Princesses, just a special dad who made his daughters feel special and let them know they were equals.

What I also remember are allowances. You were very smart in structuring our allowances based on performance and consistency. Go figure, you were a Human Resources executive. Your system instilled responsibility, work ethic, and reward reinforcement at a young age. I'll do it for my kids. A weekly checklist and then the pay out. And I loved completing them all and getting a bonus, something, by the way, that my brother and sister rarely got!

And those softball games with the neighborhood kids behind our house in Bloomfield Hills, Michigan! You and Mom always had something going on. Our parents always made time for the family activities. You were always a big kid at Halloween. We would even dress up our dog. You would always say, "Don't worry about what other people think; have fun, and be yourself."

Every New Year's Eve was a night to anticipate. Both sets of our Mimi's and Papa's plus the five of us (along with our dog, Mig—short for Amigo) played cards after dinner. Once again, you stressed the importance of family "quality time" together. Not to mention, as a kid it was awesome to have soda pop and chips (even the occasional sip of beer), stay up late, and play cards (Michigan Rummy) for pennies.

And funny that the three of us would wake in the morning and find pennies under the table, not realizing at the time that our Papa's—and maybe even our Mimi's—were up to tricks!

I loved the sing-along with you at the piano or the duets with me on the violin. Looking back, I felt like a "star," performing to you and Mimi/Papa. One of my personal favorites, and I have many, was from Annie: "Together at last, together forever." I always felt like I was Annie and that you were Mr. Warbucks!!

One of the funniest of all moments was tickling you to death after our first move to Coventry, England. The three of us literally attacked your bare feet. You screamed, "Donna, help me" to our mom. To this day, it still makes me laugh.

After moving a couple of times, we knew what the big family chats were for. You would come home and have a "moving" chat. You always had a certain look or grin so we knew to ask, "Okay, where are we going now?" or "We are moving again aren't we?" The seven moves (three countries) we made from my ages six to sixteen made a very different life for us, but you and Mom always made sure to approach it as a family positively. I often wonder now how we would have turned out had we stayed in Monroe, Trenton, or Bloomfield Hills, Michigan or in Oakville or Norval, Ontario, or in Coventry or Solihull, England. The moves taught us many things, and I know we all wouldn't be the same people today if we hadn't moved where we did and experienced different cultures. Part of the reason our family is so close, I feel, is due to the fact that we only had each other. Moving was scary, and the places were unfamiliar, with the only constant being "our family."

Traveling allowed us to see a huge part of the western world: camels in Africa where the camel jockey offered you several camels in exchange for me (ha, ha), camping in Yellowstone with the bears on the prowl, our separate (boys, girls) barricaded rooms in France after we had seen intruders on our balconies during dinner, singing as a group in the car, having you remind us of the beauty of the scenery.

When it came time for chores, Pops loved being the official army drill sergeant: "Okay, munchkins, are we ready?" The three of us would hum and haw over having to either rake, move logs to the fireplace, or clean the pool. This cut into our lounge time, TV time, or phone call time. But, I can honestly say now that it was good for us. Chores taught responsibility, "team work" (one of the over-used terms in our house!), all pitching in, maintaining a nice home to live in, and taking care of our things. Everything was about teamwork, a family working together to ultimately benefit each contributor. You stressed that as individuals give their all, the team actually accomplishes more—so that, at the end of the project, each person had more time to do what he or she wanted. And you and mom were always part of the active workers, not just the overseers. Pops did a great job of delegating. We may have fussed, but it always got done. With your skill at delegating, we learned to address it with Pops at supper clean up, working just as we did. So, he too could do supper clean up! The lesson was profound.

I don't know when I started calling you "Pops" or how it began. It is my special name for you, no one else's. Maybe it's because we have our own special relationship as father and daughter. I actually think that I started to call you Pops once I realized what an unbelievable person you really are. This isn't to say that other people aren't loved or respected if I use their regular name, but it is just different between the two of us, and I can't really explain it. It just is.

Still to this day, it blows people away when they discover that you made me Támara's guardian for a year. I was twenty and she was just seventeen when you moved to Virginia from Canada. You had promised not to move her during her high school years, at my request. So, you and Mom bought a condo for us to live in while she finished high school, and I became the legal guardian. This is definitely something that doesn't happen as the norm, but our family isn't the norm anyway. This taught both of us to grow up, be independent, and become adults. This happened because we had to set house rules and keep them. We still think to this day that the aged couple down the hall on our floor were your spies!

My brother, Tarik, would always ask: "Are we rich?" Pops would always respond that we are rich in many ways. What a concept. And now I sometimes wonder if this is why I am not materialistic.

MARVIN JOSAITIS

You always taught us values, morals, power of love, what defines them, and what defines success. I feel lucky just to reflect on some of your philosophies, because many have become mine now as an adult.

Needless to say, I really appreciate the encouragement, direction, and advice that you gave to me growing up. You were always there, along with Mom, whether it be at a softball game, studying for a test, a dilemma at school, or "boy" problems. You always listened and gave advice or encouragement to help us make our own decision, and we had to then accept the responsibilities and consequences. You gave us an awareness of budgeting our allowances or paychecks and the importance of saving. You always set high standards, encouraging us to be the best you can be.

Finally, I shall always remember our dinners in Toronto when you came for business after you moved to Virginia and I remained in Canada. These were special times to say the least. I know that I always talked your ear off. But I'd never trade them in for anything! Whether we'd chat about people, work, family, or budgets, these were and still are the best of times. Talk about feeling special.

Flash 17

On March 8, 1974, a third special new love entered my life—Támara. Her name, meaning "Palm Tree," is a popular name, especially among Russian Jews. She dictated a letter to me through her mother medium three days after her birth:

> Dear Daddy,
>
>   Mommy has been telling me all about you and my big sister. I am getting very excited about going home tomorrow. I just kept dreaming about it after Mommy told me how close it is now when I can finally meet you.
>
>   You must really be exceptionally special because you were so understanding with Mommy all the while she carried me. I was very glad that you were

with Mommy too in the delivery room … that was quite a happy welcome for me.

Mommy told me how much it meant to her to have you with her. I was glad too, 'cause I got to see you together as the first experience in my life. I liked that!

You take it easy and get lots of rest … I can hardly wait until tomorrow when we can go home together. I may be little, but I can take lots of love.

Daddy, I want to be with you and learn to love you like Mommy says you love me.

Támara xxxooo

MARVIN JOSAITIS

Flash 18

Twenty-five years later. Támara hand wrote her own contributions to my kaleidoscope memories on Father's Day, 1999:

> Dad,
>
> I started writing these "memoirs" one way, as a narrative to track through the years. But then, I realized that many of these ideas stand apart as a category and occur at a number of different parts of my life. Please forgive the change of style and the lack of editing! There is some overlap, however most of the earliest years are in the narrative, and most of the later years are within the various subtitled categories. I'm sure that I've missed some important sections, and could certainly add more

details to those that have been included, but it's not to say they weren't important or had little impact on my life. It's more a matter of the memory not surfacing during a writing moment and not wanting to write an entire book myself!

Our family, a "Leave-it-to-Beaver" family, has had many wonderful moments. I'd never trade in growing up with the "Cleavers" for anything!

My earliest memory, prior to age four, that comes immediately to mind is sneaking into my brother's crib in the yellow glow of a night light. This crib had been my security station for only nineteen months before I was promoted to a trundle bed in order to make room for my baby brother, Tarik. I probably wasn't totally ready yet, even though our faithful Mig continued to sleep on guard between the two of us. The night light permitted me to keep my eye on my former crib and its new tiny inhabitant. The crib was close to my "big bed," which felt far too big at that time as a toddler. Tarik cooperated and shifted over enough for us both to fit. In the morning I heard my dad's voice say to my mom, "Donna, she has done it again. Támara is in Tarik's crib again." Hearing those words, I realized my dad checked on us before going to work. I loved hearing the attention and fanfare surrounding my nightly conquest of Mt. Everest, managing the climb up the railing and then getting accolades for accomplishing the feat unscathed. Tarik's bed wasn't the only one I had snuck into. At some point I also snuck into my parents' bed. When they awoke the next morning, my presence was quite a surprise! It was

MARVIN JOSAITIS

the only time, however, I successfully snuck into bed with them. I soon learned it annoyed them and that I was expected to stay in my own room. For many years, sneaking into my sister's room was allowed and proved to be excellent bonding time for us.

My days in Trenton, Michigan, were spent mostly with Tarik and my mom. Although I don't have many memories at an early age, I do remember making chocolate chip cookies with Mom. She would let us pour in the measured ingredients and would always let us lick the bowl and beaters. She would also pretend not to see all the chocolate chips we picked out before the cookies were measured out on the pan. We would also get rocked and read to during the day. Mom would even agree to play school and be the student. She taught me to write my name. I clearly remember the struggles of making a capital *A*. Mine always looked as though they were tipping over, and she continued to model letter after letter. The time I made a proper *A*, she was just as excited as I.

Our days were fun and safe. Our home was always loving. While still living in Trenton, I remember getting quite sick. This experience remains quite mentally vivid still. All day and all night I continually was vomiting. My mom never left my side when I was in the bathroom (vomiting is a very scary thing for a child). She would check on me frequently whether I was resting on the couch or in bed. She called the doctor to find out what I could eat and keep down. When that didn't work, it was time for the hospital.

My dad wrapped me in an orange-striped crocheted afghan (made by Mom) and sat me on my sister's lap as we drove to the hospital. I thought it was fun to ride in a wheel chair once we arrived. However, while in the wheelchair, I hoped I hadn't hurt my dad's feeling since I had chosen to ride rather than be carried by him to my room. The choice was simply made because of the fun of the chair, yet the nurse's reaction brought about guilty feelings. I was placed in a steel cage crib. All the time I had snuck into baby Tarik's crib—now I had my own crib again, and I never had felt so scared. At night I cried for my parents. I would crawl to the end of the bed with the IV pulling to the limit and making my arm ache. I watched the program until I fell asleep—the whole time tears streaming down my face.

Every day, my dad came to visit. It felt like a full week I was there, but it was only a couple days. He brought me a pompom mouse to keep me company and some chap stick to heal my lips. I would fall asleep while he was there and open my eyes, thinking I'd see him, but awake to a nurse checking in on me. It was always disappointing and saddening. Mom came one day and brought coloring books and crayons sent in from Kateri. She told me how much she and my siblings missed me. I missed everyone, too. It wasn't fun eating popsicles without my sister and brother, but realizing they missed me also, made me feel happier and less lonely. When I went home, it was a very happy day. I was IV free and back in my safe, loving home. The desire to be in a crib was eliminated once and for all.

We first watched "The Wizard of Oz" as a family while still living in Trenton as a three year old. When the movie was over we sang the songs and were called munchkins while put to bed. Dad would mimic the wicked witch and Oz, making us laugh. However, we were also a little afraid to head upstairs, not knowing if any of the parts could be real. This was the first time I remember having silly family times that we all enjoyed…it was also when I realized from where the word "munchkin" derived. It's funny that despite the fact all three of us look eye-to-eye with my dad we are still his munchkins.

When I was four, we moved to Bloomfield Hills. I know I was four because I asked my mom the day of the move. We had spent the night at my Mimi Margaret's—I'm sure to help my parents cope with all of the other arrangements. That morning was when I learned red and pink don't match. Even though they were the colors we used to make hearts on the same page, Kateri insisted they clashed. For the rest of that day, I felt very self-conscious that I looked like a fool in the red and pink outfit I had selected. Mim (my shortened nickname for Mimi) and Mom tried to make me feel better by not making a big deal of it…but I don't think I ever wore the clashing colors together again!

The move went well from my perspective. I was given a large room that had a cool corner. We had neighbors our age, a swing set in a big back yard, and a dance floor in the basement. Tarik had the room across the hall from me (no crib), and Kateri had a yellow room with a neat closet—it had shelves on one side. She later convinced me to trade rooms with her. Her room was better—I thought it was too, because it had been hers. She claimed she needed mine because it had red carpet (or something to that effect). So, our parents moved all the furniture from one room to another. It was under the condition that this trade was for good. At some point after the trade, I realized I got the smaller room and the closet wasn't that cool. However, it was nice to be at the end of the hall since I could play there with fewer interruptions. Later on, Kateri and I tried sharing this smaller room, but it didn't work. I've always been thankful to have a room of my own since.

In this house I have many memories. We played baseball in our back yard. Everyone helped me figure out when to swing since I rarely hit the ball on my own. We used the trees for bases and always had a fun time. We would go for family bike rides around our hilly neighborhood. We would go cross-country skiing through the woods and arrive at our elementary school. We watched the Muppet's, ate popcorn, and drank "pop" on the weekends. On the Fourth of July, we would grill out, light sparklers, and spell our names in the air. We did many things together as a family. Everyone participated, and everyone had fun.

We also learned how to rake leaves while living in this house. The munchkins had to help too since "we all had to pitch in and help out," speaketh Dad. At the time, raking was a total drag; however, we were still allowed to be kids and jump in the leaves and goof off now and then. Many years later, we value teamwork and helping others out. Shared responsibility was emphasized, and it didn't matter how much whining took place. Mom and Dad didn't give in, and so we learned to uphold our share.

Allowance worked on a similar principal. We only got paid when we did our chores—as noted on a checklist we completed on our honor. It didn't take long for us to notice and comprehend, work not done meant no pay or reduced pay. Mom and Dad knew when we didn't do a job well, and it was no fun at all to see your siblings earning more money than you.

Each of us had our own special "date-day" with Dad. In the warm weather we might have done outdoor activities such as horse-riding or fishing; and in the colder weather we would see movies, go out to eat, or go shopping. What was really neat was that we—the child—chose the special day activity. Kateri and I also got some father-daughter time through Indian Princesses. We would go on weekend retreats and have meetings at a tribe member's home. The meetings we had at our home involved Mom's creative energy to help with the craft project! The times spent together certainly reinforced tolerance of others since we had some annoying people in our tribe. The weekend retreats were most memorable for me. We learned outdoor activities and the three of us would always break away from the tribe for a little bit and enjoy the setting.

We enjoyed some of these same activities on a family vacation out west. Camping with the fear of bears eating us or our parents remains quite memorable. All the car sing-alongs and the opportunity to select the tape to be played were ours. We selected Annie the most, and my parents would honor our request. We also took a trip out east. This was less memorable; however, I learned that I was not a big fan of New York City at an early age due to its congestion.

Beginning preschool was quite a traumatic event for me. It was the first time I was put on a schedule (slight loss of freedom), and I had to mingle with other children, without the support of my brother or sister. Prior to preschool, I would have my siblings, especially my sister, break the ice and help make meeting people easier. In preschool I had to do it all on my own. I screamed each time my mom dropped me off. This of course did not make meeting other children any easier. No one wants to play with a crybaby. I would do all the activities asked of me there, but didn't really enjoy myself. I truly kept to myself while I was there. Fortunately, I was allowed to drop out of the preschool program. It was so less stressful to do coloring and play games at home. It took away the feeling of not belonging and reinforced that I belonged at home, where I could do things at my own pace and in my own style.

The time I stayed at home was clearly not a waste. My mom taught me how to read, and she

Marvin Josaitis

would not let me "get out of it." If I started slacking off, she would keep me focused. We made numerous trips to the library, and we would read in the sewing room off the kitchen. The day I could read without a lot of her help was awesome. It opened a whole new world for me. It was then I could make the story come to life! I think it's pretty remarkable that my mom taught me to read and write; both are tools/skills I attempt to teach my students now.

Kindergarten was not nearly as traumatic as preschool. In fact, I remember really liking it. I was able to put my reading and writing to work, listen to cool stories, and do math from a book. It was easier to interact with people there, and I was attending the same school as Kateri. The pluses were endless. The rest of elementary school in Michigan was positive.

Before leaving Michigan, I did have to return to the hospital to have my tonsils and adenoids removed. My dad took me in the morning and sang one of my favorite bedtime tunes that he created, "Lollypops and Popsicles," until I fell asleep and was wheeled away. (This song was enjoyed greatly many nights as he tucked us into bed.) Mom came to take me home, and I remained on the couch for a while.

Getting tucked into bed was a great part of our routine. I/we would have one or both parents come and kiss me/us goodnight. They would talk or sing for a few minutes or whatever time was needed. We found comfort in knowing they would spend some one-on-one time before we drifted off to sleep.

Birthdays and holidays were spent with family. We would gather with extended and immediate family to eat and enjoy a good time. Often we rotated homes, but our get-togethers were always fun-filled.

Eating meals together was a source of comfort and great joy. Sunday lunch/dinner was always something to rely upon. We had a well-balanced and well-cooked meal and plenty of time to spend talking and catching up. When we were younger, we had all evening meals together. However, as we grew older and everyone became extremely busy, we came to expect Sunday mealtime together. It gave us all a chance to spend at least an hour together each week and eat an enjoyable meal. Healthy eating was ingrained in us. But, so too was the atmosphere surrounding mealtime. Dining was more than just good food; it was enjoying time together.

We've had many good memories in restaurants. We were taught the correct etiquette around a table. But, we also learned how fun it can be to dine out. There have been so many times others dining in the same restaurant would have preferred that our loud laughter leave the restaurant. It was in a restaurant that we found the full humor of elephant and motorcar—something that Tarik and I had been entertained by for years before.

Dad always entertained us by playing the piano. He had a special song for each of us, and we loved it when he would play "our song." I still

MARVIN JOSAITIS

find it very calming and hypnotic to watch Dad's hands move over the keys. Dad even made sure that my husband, Chris, and I had a song to listen for! I love hearing a piece that "Dad played" on the radio. Certain songs are very comforting to hear. Always when I hear a single piano, I think about my Dad.

All of us had to take at least three years of a musical instrument. That time really helped to build an appreciation of music and the arts. I often wish that I had continued to take piano lessons. I get this feeling that later on I will take some form of music lessons again.

We were also allowed to listen to any music we wanted. Often, we would play our tapes in the car as we drove together as a family. Children and parents learned to appreciate various forms of music. To this day, there aren't many people who can listen to almost any genre of music and find something to like about it. I think all three—make that five—of us can, to various extents.

Once I started ballet, after quitting the piano, Mom and Dad provided numerous opportunities for me to see live performances of ballets. This was a special treat since Kateri and Tarik never attended. I felt so special going to the theatre with both parents by myself. I knew it was a special outing to support my individual interest. Even after I stopped taking dance lessons, they continued to get tickets for musicals and other live performances.

In middle school, I had a leading role in a school play. The entire family came to see my performance. My parents had given me flowers with a card declaring me the Best Supporting Actress. I was so excited to be in the play, and they knew it and made it more special!

Growing up, our friends were always welcome to come over and play. Often, they would stay for dinner and even sleep over. Many times friends were invited to go on outings to the theatre, movies, dinner, and even a weekend ski trip. It meant a lot to have the welcomed approval.

Eventually, I came to realize that the family liked certain friends better than others—all were welcomed, but subtleties told us which friends were more liked. As a teenager, to avoid this discrepancy, I preferred having my get-togethers with friends away from the house since I didn't want everyone I knew to go through the Josaitis evaluation! Many of the acquaintances I knew wouldn't pass; I made sure they weren't met. The friends who were closer were brought over, but I rarely asked for any input if I thought there was a chance something negative could be spotted. Siblings did enough evaluating, and as a teenager, one doesn't want to hear about any negative attributes your friends may have.

We were all encouraged to play sports and enjoy sporting events together. We played softball as a family and enjoyed both live and televised MLB games together. We also went through tennis lessons and enjoyed hours of televised Wimbledon matches. As a family we also bowled, rode horses and bikes, cross-country skied, downhill skied, walked, and most recently, golfed. When one of us had a league or tournament game, at least one parent and often a sibling would attend. At a young age, we learned the value often enjoying sports for recreation and entertainment. We also learned to support other's interest and efforts.

While living in Bloomfield Hills, Michigan, there were several Saturdays that would find Dad still in bed once the kids were awake. At least two of us (Tarik and I), and often all three of us, would crawl on the bed while Mom was up and getting ready for the day. Dad would play "monster" with us. He would wake from a slumber, growling, and would tickle us. After many rounds, Dad would eventually be ready to start his day. Once he had showered, Tarik and I would go back to visit the monster while he was shaving. Tarik and I enjoyed our pretend shave—shaving cream and a razor with no blade. It was a fun time, and I was allowed to shave with the boys with few comments made!

Moving from place to place was quite challenging at times. Moving overseas to a new culture was quite interesting. However, there are three major points that stand out about our move to England: 1) We were told to do our best at school and not worry about grades. They understood the amount of adjustments that we would need. 2) Mom and Dad provided all day horseback riding on numerous Saturdays. This gave us a chance to get away from the temporary flat, enjoy the outdoors, and not do any work on the renovations on the home to which we would move. 3) Most importantly, we learned to stick together as a family when faced with difficult times. We learned from and taught each other expressions and ways of doing things. This move above many others taught us how important family truly is. Friends do indeed come and go, but family provides strength and the truest of friends.

When other times came for us to move again, input was sought from the three of us. As a family, we discussed the timing of the move back to Canada as well as the practicality of the location. We all had given our input about not wanting to return to East Oakville, which we found to be too "class conscious." It was a place we hadn't felt like we ever belonged. Dad listened and found us a beautiful country oasis in Norval, northwest of Toronto.

A few years later, once we had our dual citizenship, we began discussing another move. This time, the discussion involved not moving as a family. Kateri and I were given the option to remain in Canada—which we did. We learned all about living on our own. We did so responsibly because we didn't want to let anyone down, most importantly ourselves. We were determined to be successful in our studies, which entailed sound choices in all aspects of our lives. We had been taught well in the 17/20 years prior. We knew what we needed to do; we had the values and skills to do it. And we did!

After moving to England, the house had so much work to be done that it occupied Mom and Dad's time. While the kitchen was being gutted, we frequently enjoyed McDonald's for lunch and Chinese for dinner. As the house was nearing completion, Mom and Dad asked one day if I would

MARVIN JOSAITIS

cook the lamb roast while they finished painting. At age ten, I discovered how satisfying cooking a family meal could be. They supported my first venture and numerous others (both good and bad dishes). Family responsibilities could come at any age. There was no set timeline. Instead, they enabled us to do things in which we showed interest.

Interest wasn't shown for all chores, yet they were still expected to be completed. We dreaded the weekend mornings that were labeled for log runs, raking, or mass mowing. However, we knew that we were expected to be a team, and we completed the tasks. We did learn from these experiences. However, I really don't remember the log runs too fondly. Dad had a way of making some projects extremely serious ventures!

In England, I also learned how to knit and crochet—pastimes that I truly enjoyed. Since neither parent knew how to knit, they found a neighborhood friend who would teach me. They purchased all of my supplies and again supported my hobby. Mom was my in-house teacher for crochet, a beautiful accompaniment to knitting.

Neither Mom nor Dad has ever said anything about my lack of working with wool in recent years. Moving over to North America brought with it a world of other activities to keep us all busy. I'm grateful not to hear about what I'm not doing in my free time!

Mig was a perfect family dog. He was protective, loyal, and loving. We tried to share the responsibility of taking care of him, but I now realize that Mom did most of the caretaking. Like most children, we wanted more out of our pet, and so we started searching for other pets. Our parents enabled us to try other pets, but we had to uphold our responsibilities. We tried gerbils, a second dog, a bird for Kateri, gold fish, and bunnies; however, none of those pets lasted long for a variety of reasons.

The move to England ultimately brought about the end of our time with Mig. We were all crushed. Once our emotional wounds healed, we started asking for another dog. Our parents made a promise that we would get a dog after our vacation back to Michigan. They kept their promise. They researched the breed, and we worked together as a family to come up with a name and a code *pee* word! Again, shared responsibility was stressed as well as shared time with not one but two Lhasa Apso male puppies, Siddhartha Sidd and Shang-Ti Max. Any wonder that we just called them Sidd and Max! We certainly remembered whose turn it was to walk the "boys" in the snow and rain! Having our dogs as family dogs encouraged the team approach and truly enabled the dogs to be an integral part of the family.

Vacations were times to experience new things together as a family while having fun in the process. Our most memorable vacations were:

"Little House on the Prairie" cottage with our two Mimi's and two Papas. We fished, caught a turtle, and played Uno, all of which were fun. And the cottage was so cool for that pop culture era of the 1980s.

"Out East" where we visited hectic NYC, friends in Maine and beautiful Cape Cod: there we caught a crab! We could spend our own money on a souvenir; both my sister and I were drawn to the crystals in Cape Cod.

"Out West" where I lost my blanket at the start of the trip, and Mom and Dad made the necessary phone call to allow me to pick it up on the way home. Many parents want to break their children's security habits ... being reunited with my blanket was a glorious day! I was so thankful to have it back in my arms and feel the comfort provided by the ribbon and soft cotton. Above all, I was relieved not to get punished for being forgetful. Instead, I learned at an early age the valuable lesson about caring for my belongings. The rest of the trip was very fun. (Tarik let me borrow one of his blankets when the need arose!) We sang along to Barry Manilow, Barbara Streisand, Annie, and the Ford Motor tapes. We went horseback riding in different states (a family favorite). We ate in neat restaurants, camped in bear country, and visited friends in Oregon. Parents may rarely attempt three weeks in the car, but our parents made sure the time in the car was worthwhile. We had games to play, music to enjoy, and conversation together. Sleep in the backseat was welcome, and we knew we would be awakened to enjoy the major sites we stopped to see.

"California—First Flight!" Mimi Margaret joined us on this trip. It was another opportunity to spend time in a car and see more of the country. If we were lucky, Dad would take us on one of his famous short cuts that took much longer! On this trip, we experienced everything from the ocean to Disneyland to Tijuana, a great place to cling to your family. Like our previous trips, we did a bit of everything, saw as much as we could, and learned yet another valuable lesson: when you travel you can visit close friends and make your travels more memorable.

"Scotland"—a stay overnight in a castle, beautiful heather, and the chance to see a Scots wedding, kilts and all! Sorry Dad, it might be the only one you ever experience firsthand. Dad, being one-eighth Scots always hoped to have one of his children marry in the plaids and kilts ... it never happened.

"Wales"—holidays away from home, time with another family to mask that our extended family was an ocean away.

"European Tour"—yes more quality time in the car. By this time, I'm sure Annie was retired; however, Barbara S. was still alive and well. The major lesson taught on this trip was to appreciate the differences in both culture and architecture. We learned firsthand the importance of attempting to speak the native language—sometimes being successful and other times not. We never could quite act out *milkshake* to the folks in Belgium! And, of course, we learned how much our parents loved old cathedrals ... I now can see the beauty in them, too!

"Tunisia" This trip can best be summarized by the following highlights:

"I want a big camel to ride in the desert!"

MARVIN JOSAITIS

"I'll have the snake around my neck!"—with Mom being the only brave one.

"This meat tastes weird; is it camel?"

Endless imitations of their speech patterns. Flying ice cream at New Year Eve's Party, and finally, "How many camels was Kateri worth?"

Each of us had the opportunity to spend time with an exchange family in another country. Spending time in Italy and later again in France helped me fully appreciate another culture. I learned what they valued and how they lived first hand as well as the art of being fully respectful of any similarities and differences. Having the exchange person living with us wasn't always easy. However, our parents taught us how to open our home and welcome "a stranger" in. We had to teach teenagers about the way we lived and make sure they didn't feel isolated. My dad provided me with the second exchange opportunity to work in France while I was at the University of Virginia. Again I lived with a family and worked with the natives. It was another opportunity provided to me that I felt so fortunate to experience. It deepened my appreciation for cultural differences, including the freedoms I came to take for granted.

When I entered grade nine, my Dad sat down and helped me map out all of my courses that would enable me to complete five years of Ontario high school in slightly more than four. As each year passed, my parents attended each awards ceremony and gave me a lot of encouragement on each of my successes. They also acted as a sounding board to my many career switches and helped me see how various careers played into both my strengths and weaknesses. Before they moved to Virginia, they (especially my Dad) helped me collect information about schools. I researched schools all over Canada. Dad provided some input on how graduates were perceived out in the market. By the fall of grade twelve, I had narrowed myself to three Canadian schools and two Virginia schools. Once I had all the acceptances the next spring, I was given the opportunity to go to the school of my choice. I didn't need to make my decision according to cost, simply on the school that met my needs. So, UVA (University of Virginia) it was. The school that had more history, beauty, and spirit than any of the other schools also offered the ideal program. The choice was mine, and I felt so lucky to have been able to be so unencumbered in my decision-making.

While attending the University, another move looked likely. Mom and Dad took me out house shopping to ensure my in-state residency. Owning and managing the house was an awesome responsibility at age twenty. It toughened me up and educated me to the real world. I would never again take for granted cleanliness!

For many years, we attended the local Episcopal church. Despite the grumbling about getting up early on Sunday morning, it was a comforting routine. Our parents made sure we each had at least one Sunday outfit that we were so excited to show off. Dad would practice for the choir on our way there— the voice exercises made us all laugh. At church, we attended Sunday school, which taught us both important and occasionally lame lessons. It provided us an additional community and an understanding of why we celebrate certain holidays. For a number of years, church was nonexistent in our lives. To many of our family, it seemed unimportant, and occasionally comments were made that made it difficult for me to express that I missed attending church. Once Mom even asked if I wanted to attend a church, but I felt so embarrassed, I declined. So, I never stated my desire to attend church. Once on my own, I began attending the Episcopal church in Charlottesville. I've since realized that I could have gone much earlier. Church provides not only the sense of community, but also a sense of spiritual grounding. My parents are supportive of this, despite their lack of a desire or need to attend now. I'm sure they would have supported my going much earlier.

Holidays became synonymous with family at an early age. Any day that was special to a family member or any national or religious holiday was spent together—no questions asked. On an individual's birthday, they had the meal of their choice and the type of dessert they desired. For us, candles could be put on any dessert; we weren't limited to cake alone … thank goodness! Often our celebrations included extended family.

When we got together with extended family, we were assured of playing cards and at times a board game, but cards were preferred. Always we ate a group meal. This at times meant the division of adults and kids, but overall there was a feeling of happiness and togetherness. It wasn't until much later that extended family gatherings became strained and certain individuals' company dreaded!

I used to think it was normal for all family and in-laws to gather together. Even for both sets of grandparents to take trips together. Since "innocent childhood," I've realized just how special that was. We never heard one set talk badly of the other. We never heard one parent bad-mouth their in-laws. Love and respect abounded. For this reason, New Year's Eve was a favorite holiday. It meant we could spend time with everyone we loved so dearly, our family of five and both sets of grandparents. We would eat fondue, a meal that lasted for hours and was fried! And we would play Michigan Rummy to bring in the New Year. Before we could play on our own, each of us would rotate from grandparent to grandparent, collecting their winnings for them and paying their wagers. When we sat on either of our Papa's lap, we were allowed to sip from their beer while drinking our precious soda pop. The game would often resume the next day before our grandparents headed home.

Funny, but there were always pennies left under the table for us to find in the morning!

Whether it was a "date" with Dad, making cookies with Mom, or being tucked in at night, each of us had our own time with each parent. It provided our own time to feel like the only one who mattered. Time to be the uninterrupted focus. In addition, we had a whole weekend of individual time with each set of grandparents. Each set would teach us new card games, take us visiting to their friends, and share with us something special about themselves. We were the only grandchild for the weekend and go spoiled like no other moment.

We could use all the bubbles we wanted at bath-time and take as long as we wanted washing the dishes. We always slept with Mimi at either house, and there we learned more about their childhoods and the childhoods of our own parents through bedtime stories. Having the individualized time with parents and grandparents helped each of us define our own relationship with each.

Mom and Dad were always very open to those whom we dated. Throughout our high school and college years, they invited dates out on family events or over for dinner. Much like our friends, we could tell who was liked more than others—always subtle indicators. I'll never forget the time Dad asked Chris, a visiting friend, to help him change a tractor tire. He asked Chris rather than my both annoyed and annoying boyfriend. It still makes me laugh today! Once Chris Gordon and I became an item, I could tell how much they enjoyed his company and personality. He became one of the family even prior to our engagement. Chris enjoyed the multitude of entrees cooked for us as we visited. If he and Dad had a red meat dish, Mom and I enjoyed seafood. We all got along so naturally—it felt right.

After two and one half years of dating, the time came for Chris to ask for my parents' blessing: the request arrived via confidential letter to them on December 1, 1996:

Dear Dr. and Mrs. Josaitis,
 Before beginning this letter, I want to make sure both of you are reading this together. If you aren't, stop reading until later.

What I have to say affects you both, and it is how I would want to do it if I were telling you this in person.

Exactly two years and three months ago, your daughter and I made it "official." Although we could sense the magic much earlier, September 1, 1994 is the day we say we began dating. Since then I have enjoyed each day of this beautiful love affair, and my heart has grown ever closer to being one with Támara's. We have experienced the joy of loving one another, the sadness of losing those we love, and now the struggle between life and death with my mom.

However, it is not the recent tragedy which prompts this letter. In fact, this is a letter, which began over two years ago, the day I fell in love with Támara. And it is a letter which marks the ending of a chapter, our first one, of a romance that is truly a blessing from God. For it is time to begin a new chapter of this romance, and for that I turn to each of you.

I am writing to ask for your blessing when I ask Támara for her hand in marriage later this month. I had hoped to do this in person, but circumstances have forced me to resort to this letter. Having explained why I wish to marry Támara, I do want to briefly explain which factors have *not* influenced this decision.

Chief among these is my mother's illness. While it may seem coincidental that this letter follows so soon after my mother's seizure and discovery of a brain tumor, I made

MARVIN JOSAITIS

the decision to propose back in the summer. Unfortunately, I still needed to make sure I would have a ring. As Támara may have told you, my grandmother promised to give me her engagement ring when I found my true love. As luck would have it, her letter saying I could have the ring this year arrived only after my last visit with you.

Just days later, the seizure occurred. Although Mom already knew the plan for the proposal, I was worried that the change in events would alter my plans. (This will all be clear when I explain my plans later in the letter.) After several long talks, Mom has convinced me that I should go ahead with my plans. So, here they are.

I would love to propose to Támara on Christmas Eve. While I realize you will be in Michigan, I have several reasons for doing it then. First, it is a time when Támara will be surrounded by all of her family. I know how important family is to her, so I can think of no better time to propose. Second, I want to show Támara how deep my commitment is to her. While that can be shown in many ways, traveling to Michigan on Christmas Eve is very symbolic of how far I will go in loving her. Third, it should be somewhat of a surprise. I want the proposal to be a time and place when she least expects it.

Having told you the plans, I now will need your help. Since I will need to return home Christmas Day, I am debating whether to fly or not. Also, I will need your help in getting Támara alone somewhere so I can propose. But these are details which we can work out later over the phone. The reason I chose to write is so that you both could experience this at the same time. Because many times only one of you is home, I thought a letter would be best. Perhaps next week we can talk on the phone.

I hope that you find this to be good news. I look forward to planning some of the details with you both. Keep it a secret from everyone for now.

Love,
Chris

Not only did they give their blessing, but they helped make December 25, 1996 incredibly special for their middle child. I know how much they did to make sure the moment was everything Chris wanted it to be. Unaware, they flew him into Michigan where we were visiting grandparents so that he could surprise me with an engagement ring, made from his own grandmother's diamond ring. Chris engaged me behind my mom's high school on the bridge of a pond located there. My parents left us their car, replete with a bottle of champagne, two pewter glasses, and a beautiful message quoting a song from "Brigadoon." They walked back to my grandparent's home. It was so beautiful and dreamy!

Our engagement gift, money, and the freedom to plan a wedding of our own with no strings attached was truly wonderful. My parents told us

that this was to be our first party … not their last.
So, Chris and I did indeed plan the wedding of
our dreams and surrounded ourselves with people
near and dear to us, not using an invitation list created by anyone else but the two of us. A new par-
adigm was created for adult children. Hopefully
Mom and Dad enjoyed the lyrics of the song that
we dedicated to them. The words represent what
each set of parents taught us about love. Love is
something that you do.

Something That We Do
by Clint Black
I remember well the day we wed
I can see that picture in my head
I still believe the words we said
Forever will ring true.
Love is certain, love is kind
Love is yours and love is mine
But it isn't something that we find
It's something that we do.
It's holding tight and letting go
It's flying high and laying low
Let your strongest feeling show
and your weakness, too.
It's a little and a lot to ask
An endless and a welcome task
Love isn't something that we have
It's something that we do.
We help to make each other all that we can be
Though we can find our strength
and inspiration, independently

The way we work together is
what sets our love apart
So closely that we can't tell where
I end and where you start.
It gives me heart remembering how
We started with a simple vow
There's so much to look back on now
Still it feels brand new
We're on a road that has no end
And each day we begin again
Love's not just something that we're in,
It's something that we do.
Love is wide, Love is long
Love is deep and love is strong
Love is why I love this song
I hope you love it too.
I remember well the day we wed
I can see that picture in my head
Love isn't just those words we said
It's something that we do.
There's no request too big or small
We give ourselves, we give our all
Love isn't someplace that we fall
It's something that we do.

You're simply the best,
    Love,
    Roonie xoxo

MARVIN JOSAITIS

Flash 19

On the Josaitis side, my grandfather, Franz, was an only son. In turn, my father, Frank, was the youngest of three boys; I was the younger of two boys. Our only son, Tarik, was the youngest child; and his only son, Talan, will carry on the family name, which has been passed on through a fragile thread. Tarik, which means, "star" in classical Arabic, was born on October 3, 1975. He was the recipient of a letter from me the following day:

> Dear Tarik,
>
> Last evening at 7:30 p.m. "strange music" filled our ears: "you have a male child." You were very quiet, breathlessly quiet, waiting for Mommy and me to react, I guess. After the births of the two loveliest girls you'll ever see—your sisters Kateri

and Támara—we couldn't believe that this time a son, a third born and firstborn all in one, five-pound-six-ounce, packaged boy, would be ours. You smiled and had the most satisfied countenance a baby could have as we watched you not more than a heartbeat away. I think you could feel our pride and love bursting and reverberating throughout the delivery room. And then, a really exciting thing happened before you left us for your nursery: Mommy and Daddy held you and cradled you in our arms. First Mommy, because after all she's not only "homed" you for most of the year, but labored to bring you "out on your own." And then I held you, and that twenty seconds felt like a whole lifetime come true: I held a "star." I haven't quite sifted all of my feelings out yet, but eventually I will—and you can help me do that.

I only hope that I will be a model of a man in the same way that your mother is of a woman for your sisters. If I can, you should grow up to be one fine chap, strong and tender, firm and sensitive, open and loving. Your mother is all and more.

The nurse who weighed you and bathed you said, "This boy will be an athletic hero." She meant well. I meant to correct her, but didn't—I wanted to say, "No, he'll be a star, his own kind of star, whatever he wants to be—those are the best stars, not molded by what others expect but by responding genuinely to their own dance." I hope we will always remember to let you "become" freely, not pushing you or expecting you or demanding you to conform to our design, but rather to be open to help you develop the unique person you are. Please

MARVIN JOSAITIS

help us do that, and Tarik will be the brightest and most beautiful of his own galaxy.

Proudly and with much love,
Your dad

Flash 20

The final contribution to me on Father's Day, 1999 came from our son, Tarik:

> A few times when I was a small boy, we would go over to the Kovak's in Bloomfield Hills and take their rowboat out on their pond to fish. We would be out for the duration of the day, catching sunfish. At times Dad and I would also try to catch turtles, using a net to bring home a surprise for the girls; we were successful one time on catching a turtle. When we decided to call it a day, we got out of the boat, and I reached immediately for the chain of sunfish we caught. This is when your favorite picture of me as a five year old was taken. Another time we went fishing at another lake. We

got up at the crack of dawn, rented a boat, and started what would end up being an all day affair. I remember trolling back and forth in search of perch. After about five or six hours, your head was starting to get burnt, and it was probably time to head in. But I looked at you and said, "Just a little bit longer?" Finally when the sun started setting, I knew it was time to go.

Even as a teenager, our first morning at our pond (at the home you called Mardon Pond Hollow) was a great fishing day. We were out all morning and part of the afternoon. It was probably the single most successful fishing day we had. We were averaging a fish every five minutes. When we finally called it a day and paddled to shore, our basket of fish was overflowing. So were the memories.

I loved the weekends when I would help you cut the grass, walking in front of you, holding onto the lower bar of the lawn mower while pretending that I was cutting the grass. Whenever we had some spare time, we would also go to the back yard and play catch.

When I needed to get my tonsils and adenoids out, both you and Mom took me to the hospital late at night and stayed with me all night, all the way up until the surgery. The one memory that sticks with me is the song "Lollipops and Popsicles" you sang to me just before I was sedated.

On Saturday mornings, Mom would let me come in and lay in bed with you. The best was when you did the "monster" impersonations. After spending time in bed, we would go into the bathroom and shave together. You would have a real razor of course, but I would use a razor with no blade.

One day I remember pestering you to let me smoke a cigar that was given to you. After hours of persistence, you finally let me. We went outside, and I lit the cigar. I remember coughing after every puff. I didn't realize at the time that you let me smoke to teach me a lesson. Well, that lesson worked, because when I was done I didn't want to see another cigar or to smoke ever. I haven't to this day.

One time in Bloomfield Hills, you threatened me that you would wash my mouth out with soap if I used another cuss word. Well, I didn't listen. I remember being carried up the stairs into the bathroom and placed on the countertop; a soap bar was then jammed in and out of my mouth a couple times. I learned my lesson that day as well.

Many times at dinner when we had vegetables, neither the girls nor myself would want to eat all of them. However, before we could be excused from the table, one of you would split our vegetables up in separate piles and make us finish one of the piles. No permanent damage occurred!

One night I remember being up in my room, packing a bag in an attempt to run away from home. As I was on my way down the stairs, you were waiting for me. You asked me where I was heading. I said that I wasn't sure, just away. You followed me to the door and said that everyone would miss me very much. I simply turned around and looked at you, and you said, "Will I still be your best bud?"

I answered, "You will always be my best bud."

When we lived in Ontario, I used to love getting up early to go charter fishing with you. We would spend a half-day on the lake enjoying a little quality time, hoping to catch "the One." When the day was over, I remember returning to the dock with Mom and the girls waiting for us to see what we caught.

When I was nine, one of the many highlights from our Tunisia trip was the camel ride along the beach. What a memory to have! So many memories are difficult to write about, so what I would like to do is simply list a few: our trip to Wales golfing on the course with all the sheep, living in a small flat in Coventry England while our home in Solihull was being readied for occupancy, getting picked up by Mom in her little old ladies used Triumph Dolomite car in England, horse riding and piano lessons in England, and listening to the Lone Ranger Theme song on long road trips.

There were many times that I would go golfing with you and your friends. I would usually act as your caddie and carry your bag. If I was lucky, you would let me putt a couple times. In addition, after you would hit a great drive, I remember asking, "Will I ever be able to hit the ball as far as you?"

Quick flash from Dad: Tarik, I haven't beaten you since you turned fifteen! You put a curse on my golf game! End of mini-flash.

MARVIN JOSAITIS

Many nights we would go downstairs and have pool tournaments. A couple times we would have an audience looking through the window, our outdoor cats Romeo and Jewel. The best part of the tournament would be playing for the lucky rabbit's foot, a gift that your dad, Papa Frank, had given to me long ago. I believe what started the pool tournaments was when we were living in England at the home you called "Glen Eden." We had the pool table set up in the den, and every time we would play, I would put on the suit vest and pretend that I was a professional snooker player.

When you were the coach for my first little league soccer team, I remember that you were always fair. You played everybody equally and kept statistics so you would be able to reward the right players with gifts. One of the most vivid memories I have from that team was when our goalie went to punt the ball and accidentally kicked the ball over his head and into our own net! You were patient with him and kind. For some reason, I would always practice against our garage door. Well, as you know our family room window was right beside it. One day when I was kicking the ball against the garage, my aim was off, and the ball ended up through the window inside our living room. You also were understanding of a small boy's energy and unintentional goof.

You were another coach of mine when we were living in England and I was on a squash team. Our team would practice on Saturday morning, followed by an inter-league match. My teammates in both instances loved you as a coach. Both teams

135

PENNIES FROM A HEAV'N

were also very successful. I am extremely proud and thankful for you, "the Coach."

When I was in high school in Virginia, during soccer season, you and Mom had the opportunity of a lifetime to go to a live Barbara Streisand concert. However, you decided to watch a soccer game I had the same evening. Even though there were many other games that you attended, you decided very unselfishly to support me. You were always there no matter what sport, time, or place.

Flash 21

Reading again the memories of my youngest and only son as a young boy, my mind carries me back to the letter that Donna and I received from him as a twenty-year-old in college when he was on an imposed silence period prior to initiation into a fraternity at Elon College in North Carolina. His required task was to think about his life and write a letter to his mother and father. My best bud wrote on November 3, 1995:

Dear Mom and Dad,

I don't even know where to begin. Today is Friday. I think ritual will start today and end sometime tomorrow; that means I will be a Sigma Chi come the end of this weekend. The past six weeks has had such an impact on how I will live my life,

137

especially the past week (I-Week). I learned so much about myself and the fraternity. It is amazing how much a person can learn about himself when you take away all forms of communicating, having no TV, radio or being able to talk on the phone, let alone not being able to talk period. Sigma Chi is much more than girls, parties, and brothers; it has ideals that every brother strives for. The brotherhood shares a common bond on their beliefs. I don't expect you two to understand because you have to experience it for yourself.

Every night during I-week, they have an activity that makes us evaluate ourselves. After the evaluation, I realized there is not much I need to change in order to be more pleased with who I am. Don't worry, I am already pleased with who I am, but I can try harder to be there for family members and friends, among other things. Sigma Chi has given me values to live by; this is called the Jordan Standard:

A Man of Good Character
A Student of Fair Ability
With Ambitious Purposes
A Congenial Disposition
Possessed of Good Morals
Having a High Sense of Honor and
A Deep Sense of Personal Responsibility.

As you can see, it is a blueprint of life.

I have taken so much for granted in life. I guess it's to do with the type of parents you have been. Every time I needed someone to talk to, you were there. Every time I needed something, you supplied it for me. No matter what I do, I don't think I can ever repay you both. I can only try. At times I realize

I got short tempered and lazy, but Sigma Chi has given me the time to evaluate myself. The next time you see me, you should hopefully see a difference. The family you supplied for Kateri, Támara, and myself is immeasurable; you have spoiled us dearly with love, stability, and generosity. I wish I will be half as good a parent as you have been. At least I have *good* role models. I'm sorry for not expressing myself that much to you guys, but for some reason, I tried to hold it inside and work the problems out by myself. That only made more anger build up inside, which caused some of my mood swings. No matter what I did in the past to insult you or neglect you, I apologize and feel ashamed for it. I feel the values you showed me have only strengthened in time, especially the past few weeks. I realize we had some hard times over the past summers and before I went off to college. Please don't take it personally; I feel we need to have some bad times to appreciate the good times even more.

I would always reflect on the good times we had; I will never forget those times; they are the memories I cherish. The fishing expeditions we would do or the loud cheers you would send from the stands will always be remembered dearly. Thank you for everything you did for me with golf. I realize the time and money spent on those golf tournaments where I played were immense. I really do appreciate that time spent with you two at Virginia Beach and all the other high school golf tournaments. I can't even tell you what you mean to me, nor can actions show enough. The only thing that realizes how much you mean to me is my heart. The weird haircuts, the earring, plus anything else weird that I have done were all stepping-stones to try and find out who I am. I think I have found it: I am a man of good character, as stated in the Jordan Standard.

I feel I should be honest with you two even more than I have been. Throughout the past few years, I have started to drink. At parties, it is much more fun to have a few drinks with everyone. I am much more relaxed in that kind of situation with a few beers. Don't worry. I won't be an alcoholic, as I see how that affects people. Also, my accounting grade is awful. No matter what I say or anybody else says, my professor still teaches horribly. He is one of those teachers whose teaching ethic I have a hard time comprehending. I am trying, but it is very frustrating, so much so that at times I feel like crying. However, when I am struggling in accounting, I have found something within myself that will benefit me for life.

I realize I was rambling, but there is so much to say, I still have much more to say, but words won't capture half the meaning:

I will always love you both forever.

No matter what my actions portray, I mean the best for you both.

I miss you and constantly think about you.

Thank you for everything.

I miss the times when I was dependent on you both and would spend quality time together with you.

Love - Tarik

Marvin Josaitis

Flash 22

The Hallmark cards my three munchkins sent me in 1999 for Father's Day in addition to their written memories from childhood days were the following verses.

> With Love from your Daughter Kateri: Pops,
>
> You're an extraordinary man, a man whose example inspires me, a man who was my very first hero. I can't tell you how often you are my encouragement to be brave, my permission to be silly, my gentle push to listen to my own intuition. So much of the woman I have become has been influenced by all you have been to me—and as you celebrate today, know that I am celebrating everything that makes you the loving father and friend you are.

Lots of Love from Roonie (and Chris):

As strong as the rhythms of nature, the strength of a father's love. Today is filled with special thoughts of all the days you fill with love.

Tarik's:

Father's Day is a chance to express wishes for love and happiness—warm and special wishes that too often go unsaid. Sometimes we get so busy that the time just slips away, and we forget to mention all the things we want to say—and so this wish is being sent as just a little token of thoughts and wishes often felt but all too seldom spoken.

I have come to the conclusion that pennies in my life come and have come in many forms. Some are copper coin, and others are golden words beyond transactional value, often called pearls of wisdom. The latter are the most valuable in the end. Both are pennies, one actual and the other symbolic, memories from a respective heav'n.

Over the years, each of my children in their uniquely beautiful ways has showered me with too many pennies to count.

MARVIN JOSAITIS

Flash 23

It may appear at this point that my family centers around me. Quite the contrary. The heart of the Josaitis family at its core is Donna, my companion in making family. On behalf of our three children, Támara expressed the reality best, shortly after the Father's Day of 1999:

> Mom,
>
> When we presented Dad his Father's Day gift, we had focused many of the memories on him. So many of these memories reflected family experiences that we were all a part of. You also would have read some individual tributes to you. I wanted to address this letter to you to identify some key aspects you had in our growing up.

Mom, you were the often-quiet cement that held us together through thick and thin. You stayed home with us when Dad travelled. Despite the one ice cream cone incident, where you got so upset with our silliness at the dinner table once in England when you threw the cone at us, you constantly reinforced for us the importance of quality in the time we spent together—not quantity. I'm sure there are many spouses that start talking badly of the other who is away and how much work they are left to take care of around the nest alone. We never heard any of that from you. Instead, we admired his hard work and all the things he did to provide the best for us. We knew of no resentment.

In addition to always being around, you drove us to and from all of our extracurricular activities and friends' homes. You did all the necessary stitching for ballet garments and sport clothes. You learned how to put hair up in a bun to meet the strict standards of the ballet instructor as well as any expectations or standards from any of our teachers or coaches. Undoubtedly, tending to all the running around, housework, and the unexpected meant that you had little or no time for yourself. Even during times of cleaning the house ever so deeply to rid it of lice or other varmints, you still supported rather than grumbled. You took care of the situation and comforted. We even learned to identify your emotions through the tonality of your expressions.

All the hard work was one thing, but you also managed to put some fun times in there, too. Playing school, making cookies, crocheting, aerobics, and so-

MARVIN JOSAITIS

cial moments. You provided us quiet times to ourselves and taught us to respect when others needed to enjoy their time alone. You taught us how to have balanced lives with an admixture of play and work. You always played along during our imaginary playtime. Whether it was pretending to run a restaurant, acknowledging the needs of our "pets and babies," having speed-walk races, or bike races, you validated our games. The list could go on and on.

Reflecting upon our childhoods, it is clear to see how much teamwork goes into parenting. It is also clear to see the importance of being unified and loving unconditionally. With all of our moves, it is fair to say that much of what you did helped us become more stable in our new environments and adapt to changes in our family life brought about by changes in the demands of Dad's job.

This is just to let you know that you did an incredible amount for us that we often don't tell you we recognize. Once you share this with Dad, he can use it as more research for his writing. You two make an unbelievable team.

Thanks for everything!

Love,

Hugs and kisses as well,

Your three munchkins

Flash 24

In our family, our children have always pointed out correctly that Donna, my spouse and best friend, was and is today the integral part of making our family. If I was the head, she was the heart. Together we made it. Together we continue to make it. Without each other, family for us and our children, their spouses, and grandchildren now part of that reality would be missing a link, an essential element. We cherish that "making." We also have called that "becoming married," an active process rather than a static reality.

Donna continues to make family by crocheting gifts, having special moments with each of our six grandchildren, and always ending the encounter with, "Don't forget I love you." Pennies have come from the expressions, twinkling of grandchildren's eyes, and heartfelt thank yous. A most beautiful moment came about two years ago when our grandson, Talan, was complimented by a woman for the beautiful crocheted sweater he was wearing. Not quite three at the time, he patted the sweater with both palms and with much pride slowly and carefully said, "My Mimi made me!" What pennies from a heav'n!

Through Donna as well as me, we continue to "make family" together. We know it, but—more importantly—our three kids, their spouses, and six grandkids know it as well.

Flash 25

Little has been written here regarding my father's family. Little is worth recording. If there is a sadness in the total making of family, this is that. I had little contact with my Josaitis uncles, aunts, and cousins until my teenage and young adult years. And even then, the contact was sporadic with a sense of the tensions that had been created years before my birth. Families, unfortunately, can have disagreements and differences of values that cause the members to break apart. Frequently, the final break comes when the parents die. There are no easy formulas to fix broken families. At times, over many years, the reasons for the breaks or the hurts are not even remembered fully or accurately. It happens.

This happened within my father's family. As a consequence, my father and his siblings attempted—but not with total success—to mend what was broken for too long. Civility ultimately occurred, but not familial warmth. As a consequence, I experienced infrequently and too late in youth a part of my heritage where bonded warmth and commonality of purpose didn't exist. This bitter and sad chapter in my life has permitted me to conclude that when this happens, sometimes the best part of valor is letting go and getting on with more meaningful relationships. It is best to make no excuses in the process. And it is even better to carry no remorse, anger, or bitterness. As Eleazar ben Judah proffered nearly eight centuries ago: "The most beautiful thing man can do is to forgive."

Flash 26

When I met Donna Marie Rimer on a blind date/dance July 5, 1969, my experience both in dating and dancing were minimal at best. Perhaps the word *primitive* describes it more accurately. I had just resigned from the Catholic priesthood a month earlier after having spent twelve faithful "no-dating" years preparing in the seminary. A former parishioner introduced us that evening in Toledo, Ohio, a quick jaunt from Monroe where Donna had lived most of her life and where I would be starting a new career as a college instructor. Little did either of us expect that on our second date fifteen days later, we would be watching Neil Armstrong's walk on the moon, a symbolic prelude to the marvelous journey we would soon begin ourselves.

Exactly three months later on October 5, 1969, we had decided to drive to a lake ninety minutes west of Monroe in what was popularly called the Irish Hills. We stopped there to climb a stately willow tree, a sport that Donna particularly fancied. While we sat in the tree, hanging over the shoreline, I handed her a small box. In it was a delicate pearl ring encased in silver. Donna gasped: "What is this?"

I stammered, "Well, when a guy gives his girl a ring, it usually means that he is asking her to marry him." A skillful tree climber, Donna nearly fell from the willow! True to our close family upbringing, we decided that no answer could be definitive until the future bride's parents approved and gave their blessing. We quickly departed the tree and drove back to Monroe to share the news and pose the question.

Asking Gerald and Ada (Reau) Rimer the simple question was easy. They were the type of informal, mid-western people who made it easy. The three months of courtship had given me an opportunity to establish a comfortable relationship with two wonderful people, not unlike my own parents. Jerry, as he was called, even resembled my own father. Each fell a couple of inches shy of six feet with trim, albeit not athletic, frames. Both were fair skinned with grey thinning hair and grey-green eyes that came alive when any of their progeny entered the room. Often, the two of them were asked if they were brothers; even their quiet disposition seemed to support the suspicion. Our parents were so similar in interests and values that, after our two families were bonded, the four of them later would even vacation together.

After I asked for their daughter's hand in marriage to a shocked pair, Donna's father excused himself for a private conversation with his daughter. Donna's mother and I made small talk in the meantime. When father and daughter returned to the living room, the bright happy look on their faces told the answer. The affirmative words that followed were unnecessary but welcomed by a slightly nervous twenty-seven-year-old engaged young man staring at his slightly nervous twenty-two-year-old fiancée. Donna was their eldest of three and the first to marry. So all of us were slightly nervous!

We were married in Monroe the following March 25, 1970, in a small candlelight ceremony attended by our closest forty family and friends. A reception for three hundred followed. Donna began a beautiful tradition that evening by being married in her mother's wedding gown, wearing a gold cross that her mother, her Mimi Reau, and her Grand-Mimi Valequette all had worn at their weddings. When our daughter Támara was married, she was the third generation to wear the same dress. Since 1941 and every 28-plus years later, a Reau, Rimer, Josaitis has walked down the aisle in the same, simple, white, satin dress—unfaded over the decades—merely slightly adapted to meet stylistic differences. Mom Rimer lived to see her granddaughter replicate the memories of 1941 and 1970 in 1998. "What is a family, after all, except memories?"

Dad and Mom Rimer were second parents for me. Donna felt the same about my parents. Her father was a gentle and quiet man who had similar qualities to my father. He generally had a pipe in his hand and enjoyed

spending time conversing, playing cards with us, or helping us by sharing his talented handyman and carpentry
skills. Mom was a very practical and honest person who
also loved our company. Her home was our home. Her
time was our time. Her mothering skills became loving
grand-mothering skills when we presented her with her
first grandchildren to love. It was wonderful to have new
parents who accepted me as their older son.

While Dad was an only child, his stepbrother—Owen
Scott along with his wife Eunice—in nearby Ohio welcomed me as a new nephew. Mom's family had lived in
Monroe for two centuries. Her mother Cecilia Reau,
Donna's Mimi, who still lived only a block away, became
my new Mimi. It was wonderful for me to have a Mimi
again after more than two decades without. I now also
had many new uncles, aunts, and cousins. The Reau and
LaPrad families accepted me into their families, remarkable especially since I had months before been functioning
as a priest in their community—and a rather conservative
community at that. Mom and Mimi, I am told, were frequently asked what it was like having a former priest in the
family. They would just shrug and say simply that it was
like having another wonderful son or grandson to love.

While our first home was an apartment twenty-five
minutes north of town, we eventually moved into town
after our first year of marriage and established ourselves
a block away from Mom, Dad, and Mimi Reau. Until
we were able to purchase our first home when it became
vacant across the street, Mom and Dad Rimer were our
landlords. What a wonderful environment to raise our

three babies for their first six years of life. They and we were rooted in a community where nearly all of Donna's family lived. So our young family lived and experienced a four generational reality during their formative years. For our young children, their Papa Gerald, Mimi Ada, and their one Grand-Mimi lived just a block away with Papa Frank and Mimi Margaret less than an hour by car.

Mom and Dad Rimer had married in Monroe, Michigan, three months and a week before I was born. Like my parents, death ended a beautiful and long marriage fifteen months prior to their fiftieth anniversary. As a consequence, our children have come from several generations of long marriages. In truth, we don't know of any divorce in either of our direct lineages.

We were so fortunate to have Mom and Dad's constant love and support in our own marriage. I was fortunate to have them as dear friends as well as nouveau parents.

What memories they, along with my parents, gave to our children who distinguished their four grandparents by adding the given name of each to Mimi or Papa. In effect, the joy of making family began with them and was rekindled through them with our three munchkins.

Flash 27

Throughout our marriage, our anniversary dinner has been a sacrosanct moment when we have dined at a special place. Our children have known that we can replay from memory each restaurant where we have been to celebrate the year and what we ordered at each and every restaurant, despite the fact that, in their shorter married lives, where they celebrated last is often a question mark! Donna and I have a ritual of re-living each of the forty-one anniversaries to date by place and type of meal. We do this at every anniversary celebration. Maybe it is our way of proving to ourselves that Alzheimer's has yet to take hold! Virginia has hosted thirteen of our anniversaries; Michigan—where it all started—has been the place for eleven of our celebrations; Ontario is third with eight,

England fourth with three, and New York, California, Ohio, West Virginia, Maryland, and Puerto Rico sharing the rest. All have been celebrations with Donna and me being the only participants with a couple of exceptions. Our baby Tarik—due to nursing—shared the honors early in our married life on anniversary six. By exception, he, along with his spouse Archana, and his son, Talan, also shared our celebration on anniversary thirty-six.

Hence, it was a surprise to our eleven treasures (our youngest grandchild, Eesha Rimer Josaitis was not yet conceived) when we announced in early 2009 that we wanted to make our fortieth year of marriage culminating on March 25, 2010, a year filled with memories inspired by Judd's previously acknowledged "What is a family, after all, except memories?" It was a surprise to them that we wanted this year to stand out as an attestation of the joy of making family.

Rather than have a secluded, once-in-a-lifetime trip that only the two of us could tuck in our memory banks, we have had several trips and significant time together with our children and grandchildren during this "ruby" year. In all of our memories now, distinguished only by our own interpretations, were a Memorial weekend spent together at Niagara Falls, Ontario, a Christmas weekend in the most magical of Holiday Towns—New York City, and the fortieth anniversary dinner in Virginia where we have celebrated our most.

Niagara came first since it is such a wondrous blend of the natural augmented by the human. The trip became an especially anticipatory time for Kateri and Dan to introduce their three-month-old son Jackson for the first time to his awaiting two aunts, two uncles, and four cousins. Donna and I had met him shortly after birth. Whilst I had become used to being a Papa to our American grandchildren, we asked if our new Canadian grandson could greet me as his Pipi, tying him through me to his Canadian great-great grandfather, my Pipi whom I had never met, and to the generations of Canadians in our family before him.

The first major event for everyone now in Niagara Falls, Canada, was the chance to finally cuddle the new "bubúne" of the Josaitis family who was busy absorbing through his own young and vibrant goggles on life. Their "me-first" fervor almost led them to pick numbers, determining the order as each prepared outstretched arms for the first cuddle. Adults and kids were indistinguishable in their excitement! Mimi and Pipi autocratically decided that it would be fair to begin with the eldest and work down to the youngest who had just graduated from being the "bubúne," a position he had held for three years. Now cousin, Adestan, was a big boy proudly handing on the honor, the diploma, to his cousin Jackson. These first moments with Jackson were tender, warm, and beautiful. We were the Josaitis, celebrating our fortieth together as a family.

Niagara Falls permitted all of us dressed in rain gear to experience the wonder of Niagara together at the base of the mist from the deck of the Maid of the Mist, except for Talan who, by his own choice, was the wettest of all. Our grandchildren's eyes were larger than ours as the boat pulled within yards of the cascading Horseshoe Falls.

From there, we followed the Niagara on foot through the gorge, witnessing the only level-six, white-water rapids in the world. And then, the thirteen of us continued down the gorge via the tramway across the whirlpools, looking back toward where we had been. Everyone was awestruck at the natural beauty that, too often, is taken for granted as "touristy." At night, it was atop the Skylon Tower, overtaken by the fireworks' display decorating the backdrop of glowing Falls dressed in the colors of the rainbow. Along with the Maid of the Mist and the first holding of Jackson, the night display from stories above the gorge were the favorites of our three oldest grandchildren: Mackenna, Cailean, and Talan.

All meals were together. All events were together including a day at Marine Land. I, of course, will never forget holding one of our three-year-olds—Adestan—as we watched the killer whale show. Around and around the whales swam. I was telling him to keep watching. And, unexpectedly, I turned away from the whale by natural instinct forgetting that the grandson in my arms would bear the brunt of the spray head-on. Indeed, he was overwhelmed by a wave of salt water in his face, compliments of a killer whale swimming near our barrier. Adestan has buried the memory, I am sure.

Six of the adults, including me, went on their version of a wicked roller coaster, which is wicked and which brought back many memories of the past. At my age, I wasn't sure whether I would replicate that joy again!

My family still reminds me of my lying down on a park bench for a nap at Marine Land, giving the impression of

MARVIN JOSAITIS

being a homeless derelict—but the events had caught up with me, and I did it hoping that no one would put a hat near me with a donation sign. In between, our children and their spouses were able to get caught up and also reminisce about their lives growing up in Josaitis' land—then and now.

On Christmas Day, New York City decided it wouldn't be outdone. Everyone "AMTRAKed" together to the Big Apple, three from Syracuse, New York, and ten from Washington, DC. We stayed minutes from Times Square and allowed ourselves to be entranced by the city's best charm, the holiday season.

Highlights for everyone: Radio City Music Hall Holiday Extravaganza with the Rockettes still kicking in our memories, a tour of the new Yankee Stadium for the guys while the girls lunched and re-lived youth with our only granddaughter at the time, Mackenna, at the American Girl store. Other memorable events included: Central Park by horse-drawn carriage, Times Square at night with the mimes, a pedicab trip to an evening meal where Donna and I plus Mackenna, Cailean, and Adestan arrived on our laps with our other children and grandchildren running out wondering what had taken us so long, wonderful meals accommodating all food allergy needs, and the opening of Christmas presents around the tree in the lobby of our weekend home at the Grand Hyatt. At ten months of age, Jackson again held center court with everyone!

Donna and I watched sleeping grandchildren in the evening whilst our children re-lived the current and past memories of family. We were the Josaitis clan, celebrating our fortieth together as a family.

The trip was signaled from a heav'n. As we exited the cab back to one of the AMTRAK trains ready to return ten of us to Virginia, I looked down: between the curb and the open cab door lay a shiny dime! As I picked it up, I thought of my mom.

Throughout the year, we have had other memorable events. We had a four-day trip to Disney World with Támara's family, a surprise trip to Ontario to celebrate the first birthday of our grandson Jackson, complete with a smearing of his face eating his first chocolate cake and taking his first steps. Other significant time was spent with Talan prior to his entering full-time day care. We have watched with joy our children loving every minute of the daily excitement that comes from watching their children experience new things, some for the first and last time. We have loved seeing our granddaughter moving close to puberty, yet still living the excitement and thrill of the last glows of childhood; when we take her to the theater or watch her ballet, the artist in her bubbles forth. We have loved the beautiful boyhood years with all of its new thrills and experiences of Cailean playing baseball or dancing on stage, of Talan and Adestan growing together out of toddler-hood, and the freshness of our one-year-old Jackson as he experienced for the first time what his cousins and parents did before him. We have and do see it all, for we are the Josaitis celebrating our fortieth together as a family.

MARVIN JOSAITIS

Flash 28

At our celebration in Niagara Falls, our family presented us with a framed picture created by Kateri on behalf of all: a willow tree with the appropriate birthstones of each of our thirteen family members (our sixth grandchild, Eesha, born December 6, 2010 will be honored with the four-teenth birthstone) gracing three of its distinct branches! Above the willow tree are the words:

> *It started in a tree*
> *with a pearl*
> *And look how it's grown*
> *after 40 years....*

The plaque now graces our dining room buffet center stage.

Flash 29

Kateri, Dan, and Jackson—due to work commitments—
were unable to be with us in Virginia to celebrate the
conclusion of our fortieth year of celebrations on March
25, 2010. However, we had traveled to Canada to be with
them earlier in the week. They left us a Hallmark card
message to take to the celebration that summarizes as
completely and beautifully as they could our forty years
of making family. Needless to say, Donna and I did not
have dry eyes as we opened their gift to us that night.
And to our disbelief and without any prior collusion on
their parts, quite unexpectedly like pennies from a heav'n,
Támara, Chris, Cailean, Mackenna, and Adestan had
picked out the same Hallmark greeting:

The story of our family
is made up of many things—
from silly jokes
to good-night kisses,
from nicknames
to summer vacations,
from hard good-byes
to the most joyous homecomings.
The story of our family
is made up of love
and time
and memory . . .
all the things that really matter.
And at the heart of our story
will always be
the two of you.

Marvin Josaitis

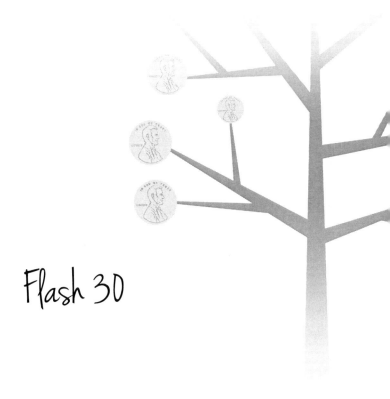

Flash 30

The presence of our children and grandchildren at our fortieth anniversary celebration was gift enough. But, in addition, on behalf of all of them, Archana had worked diligently in getting the pictures that encapsulated the memories of that year spent together in Niagara and New York City into a bound book, entitled *Memories—Our 40th Anniversary Celebration!* She was not even aware that I was writing a family memoir that focused on Judd's theme, which so aptly describes a family: "For what is a family, after all, except memories."

The twenty-eight-page volume of *Memories* begins with a family photo of the thirteen of us and then traces our memory-filled fortieth through Niagara from the Maid of the Mist through the Bird Kingdom and our walk along the Niagara Gorge and our day together at Marine Land. Then, it is on to the "Big Apple" for Christmas at the Grand Hyatt, the fabulous restaurants, the Radio City Music Hall Spectacular, Rockefeller Center, the pedicab ride, horse-drawn rides through Central Park, and the boys' tour at the new Yankee Stadium while the girls lunched and dreamed at the American Girls Café and Store. "Memories" ends with a photo of our five grandchildren, those priceless treasures who, along with the most recent birth of our sixth grandchild, will carry on our family through the twenty-first century and beyond.

Memories now has a pre-eminent position on the coffee table in the center of our Great Room next to the wood-carving that Donna and I bought nearly two decades ago at the northern rim of the Grand Canyon; the carving is a Native American exquisite and unique rendition of family generations through the sculpture of a young brave who, as the sculpture is turned, ages in time depicting the flow of life's cycle from youth to old age. Nestled nearby is another photo album of our son's wedding on May 25, 2003, to Archana Rao, a woman of Asian Indian heritage.

Flash 31

Our son's marriage reinforced the international character of our family. Donna in a sari and I in a kurtha pajama were immersed in a Hindu wedding ceremony as defined in the Vedas, the sacred Hindu scriptures that originated about thirty-five centuries ago. Performed in the ancient language of Sanscrit, the language of Hindu Scriptures, the ceremony is rich beyond belief with enduring family and spiritual values. Their ceremony was a three-hour modern American adaptation of what would normally be a six to eight-hour ceremony in India.

The western world would do well to consider the symbolism contained in the wedding ceremony.

Family and friends gathered initially as the bride's family—the Rao's—welcomed Tarik and his family, including relatives and friends, by honoring him and me, the symbols of our family, with flower garlands at the entrance of the temple. We then proceeded into the temple to await the arrival of Archana, the bride.

Archana was accompanied into the temple by her maternal uncle to the "Mantap"—the place of ceremony—where her parents were waiting with Tarik and us as the priest invoked the memories and blessings of her father, grandfathers, and great grandfathers. At this time, a very thin, white veil was held across Tarik's face, shielding him from seeing Archana as she walked in, clothed in a fourteen-pound sari, jeweled and decorated beyond belief. The veil signified that two separate individuals would be united as one.

Five married couples then formed a circle around Tarik and Archana with a symbolic thread. This thread was used by our children to tie a band around each other's wrists. The sanctified yellow thread became as it were a protective cord, warding off any evil influences.

Archana's parents then "gave away" the bride to our son. Her father, Kudlige Rao placed Archana's right hand into the right hand of Tarik, offering her hand in marriage and asking him to promise to treat her as his "equal partner."

Tarik then tied a gold pendant (Mangalya), strung on yellow thread around the neck of his bride, Archana, in three knots. The three knots represented the Holy Trinity or the three gods—Brahma (Creator), Vishnu (Protector), and Maheshwara (Destroyer) of the Universe. This Mangalya formed the symbol of their unity. While the priest chanted the Vedic hymns to invoke the blessings for health, prosperity,

MARVIN JOSAITIS

and well being of Archana and Tarik, they festively showered each other with turmeric-coated rice.

Then, an offering of a special grain (called laja) was presented by the couple into the fire. Archana's brother Harish poured the grain from his hand into her joined hands, and then Tarik and Archana offered it to the gods. She then prayed for Tarik's long life.

Now the Saptapadi (the exchange of vows) took place. In this ceremony, Tarik and Archana took seven steps and walked around the sacred fire holding hands, symbolizing the seven sacred vows:

The first step was for respect, honor, togetherness, and prosperity; the second to develop emotional and physical health and strength; the third seeking blessings for the longevity of their life together; the fourth to always acquire knowledge, happiness, and harmony through mutual trust and love; the fifth to seek blessings for healthy children; the sixth to enjoy cheerful seasons together; and the seventh step to symbolize mutual love, friendship, and companionship while remaining lifelong partners.

For Donna and I, perhaps the most moving parts of the ceremony were twofold:

a) At one point we were invited by Archana's parents to the dais, where we were officially given Archana as our daughter to take care of and love as they had during her lifetime: we were now bound as joint parents with them for life. We were now joined to the Rao family. We were now Josaitis-Rao in assuring that their daughter, Archana, and our son, Tarik, would be part of a new family tradition carrying on the heritages of both, and

b) At the end of the ceremony Archana's parents—our co-parents—showered us with the gifts of nature: fruits and grains, symbolic of the one family that now existed in providing health and well-being to our mutual seeds: Tarik and Archana.

The entire emotional experience brought home what Archana had been telling us: family for her incorporates spouse, children, parents, brothers, sisters, grandparents, aunts, uncles, cousins (first, second, third—doesn't matter because they are all cousins), nieces, nephews, and in-laws. For her, the term "extended family" is something that has never felt quite right. "Family" in itself stands for a unit, people that share a bond together and people who are there for each other no matter what. "Extended" has never defined concepts of family as lived and experienced in the Hindu tradition.

This ancient, mystical religious ceremony fulfilled half of the wedding celebrations, the religious half. That evening, an outdoor civil ceremony witnessed by a justice of the peace took place with everyone in the wedding party dressed in traditional western formal attire, replete with a string chamber ensemble, bridesmaids, and ushers, and our three-year granddaughter, Mackenna, as the flower girl dramatically and methodically dropping petals on the carpet, awaiting the wedding party. This ceremony not only fulfilled the legal requirements but symbolized for us and all participants in both ceremonies that East had met West and at that juncture became one, indistinguishable from their two distinct cultures. The day and evening were resplendent with beautiful memories and symbols.

MARVIN JOSAITIS

The evening dinner reception was international in its composition and its beauty. We were two family traditions representing worlds apart, but together celebrating the joining of two of earth's finest harvest into one family.

So Josaitis is now bound with the "Rao" family from India in moving forward. Talan and his sister Eesha bring rich traditions from three continents together in making family as we move through the twenty-first century. The Josaitis tradition is enriched by this union of distinct families from various parts of the globe.

I suspect that our six grandchildren will have similar lifetime feelings when Donna and I are no longer contributing to their lives' memories. Maybe it is more accurate to say that I hope so. The difference will always be that each of them has known four special grandparents whereas I knew only one. The difference also is that only two of our grandchildren—Talan and Eesha—live in a three generational family under the same roof as both Donna and I had. Eventually, their experiences in some way may mirror mine with my Mimi.

And so our *Memories* takes its place on the coffee table gracing the center of our home with their wedding volume close by.

Flash 32

After forty magnificent years of marriage, replete with memories to last many lifetimes, I can only express it with the beautiful lyrics of Barbara Streisand's song, "Have I Stayed too Long at the Fair." My liberties with the lyrics are in italics:

> I wanted the music to play on forever
> Have I stayed too long at the Fair?
> I wanted the clown to be constantly clever
> Have I stayed too long at the Fair?
> The merry-go-round is beginning to slow now
> Have I stayed too long at the Fair?
> The music has stopped and the
> children must go now
> Have I stayed too long at the Fair?

The merry-go-round is beginning to taunt me
Have I stayed too long at the Fair?
There's everything to win
And there's family to want us
We've not stayed too long at the Fair.

For Donna and me, the music continues to play on forever with our beautiful family and each other. We look forward to our continued time at the Fair. We don't think that we've stayed too long. Indeed, families create memories, and at the end of the day that is what we have left: memories.

 MARVIN JOSAITIS

Flash 33

Looking back at our individual lives and our life together in kaleidoscopic fashion, Donna and I realize how unbelievably blessed and fortunate we have been. Little wonder that we want the music to play on forever! So many pennies from a heav'n have come our way—gifts from parents, grandparents, relatives, friends, and teachers who have all contributed to the charmed lives we live. Truly, we were raised by a village of caring people, the most important of which have been duly highlighted throughout these flashes.

Beginning with my birth at the very end of 1941, my memoir weaves its way to the winter of 2010. The story—my story—proudly relates the joy of living in and with functional families, a reality, sad to say, that too many people today never experience. The popular press might suggest that agony in life overshadows bliss, but this was not and is not my life. The reality for the Josaitis family, whose various colored beads have evolved into this pictorial, is as real as I have described it. To add the sordid or the unmanageably painful would have necessitated fabrication on my part. Put simply, without any apologies, my story is an involved, complex, happy narrative that has happy endings.

Maybe it is too self-centered or too romantic to think, to hope, that perhaps someday *Pennies from a Heav'n* will have new memories added to its tome by the fingers and imaginations of the youngest members of our family. Fortunately, like their parents and grandparents, to date they are also leading charmed lives. While taking his evening bath two years ago when he was still six, our eldest grandson, Cailean remarked to his mother: "I really love my life, Mom!" It is a moment like that that gives us the hope that the life, as Donna and I have been privileged to experience and fashion it, is being passed on to those who will continue to reflect and remake anew the Josaitis family through their own wonderful journeys. Perhaps they may even choose to write their memoirs someday as they look back over their evolving lives within their unique kaleidoscopes.

Throughout my seven decades, the power, the beauty, and the influence of nature have been paramount. Donna and I have learned from nature and have taught our children to appreciate, as we have, that humans are a part of and not apart from nature. I had personally learned so much of this

MARVIN JOSAITIS

from my decades at "the Lake," and during my paramour days spent climbing willow trees with Donna.

Maybe these varied flashes explain why, in early 2006, Donna and I bought a vacation home away from home, our "log haus." This exquisitely crafted rough-hewn hearth-stone log haus is perched on a hill overlooking the pristine 160-acre Alpine Lake in the Allegheny Mountains of West Virginia. Despite its logs, our "Alpine Haus" is not as primitive as the enchanted cottage that dominates so much of my memories. But its charms and character caused Donna and me to have one of those petulant love-at-first-site moments, which continues whenever we enter our new magic kingdom. The lake with its beach, its picturesque stillness as it nestles below Snaggy Mountain, and the wooded splendor around its banks all combine to provide the best of nature's elixir of love. What a place to golf, to hike, to tennis, to cross-country ski, to kayak, to canoe, to fish, to swim, or to relax with friends or family. What solace to quietly read by the fireplace on a chilly day or swing on the porch overlooking the shimmering lake and dream or reminisce! What a place to share with friends and relatives. But most importantly, what a place to tie together who we are with the most important twelve lives in our family. What a place to continue making family!

Our grandchildren love going to our log haus. It is their magic kingdom and adventure land re-orchestrated in my memory as a revival of a tune played long ago at "Portage." Unfortunately, the organized summer activities and demands on youth today with the fast pace of living—so different from my earlier days, and the more than three hour drive one-way limit the frequency of their visits. Donna and I are only hoping that their days there will attain the quality heights to permanently reinforce the values that the village once gave us to give, in turn, to them.

Some year we plan on celebrating Thanksgiving Day—one of our favorite family get-togethers—there as the fire dances at the hearth and the deer congregate near the log shed. We will watch with joy six grandchildren feeding corn to the first inhabitants of Alpine Lake who now joyfully share their place with us. And we will remember the active years of making family, complete with the beautiful memories that only a family can make.

Who knows? Perhaps our six grandchildren may even tell generations yet to come about those special moments that they experienced at "the Lake," those special once-in-a-lifetime treasured moments that they shared with their only Mimi and Papa (or Pipi) at the enchanted log haus on the hill.

Flash 34

Alice Roosevelt Longworth, the eldest child of President Theodore Roosevelt, is attributed with many witty quotes during her life that spanned nearly the entire twentieth century. One of my favorites: "At first you're young, then you're middle-aged, then you're wonderful." I have arrived at the beginning of "wonderful"! Donna is just behind me. Now we are able to appreciate the families that have made us who we are and, at the same time, we have contributed to the making process in so many ways. Our ancestors, friends, and neighbors, along with collected sages of history, have fashioned this family man in ways as numerous as the stars. Youth, middle age, and now "wonderful," all merge and continue to interplay, interspersing reality with memory.

As a teenager, my brother and only sibling, Norman, wrote in a poem that he entitled "Innocence Grown Wise" what I still dream for myself, but now also dream for our children and grandchildren as they continue to make family:

Are you still so small a blade of grass
Can whisper in your ear?
Or a lupine for your looking glass
Make wonders of it clear?
Do magic movements of the sea
Wave Isles before your eyes?
Elysium where your mind can flee
As new horizons rise?
In that garden of the sky I'd run
With playmates who were stars:
We'd play hide go seek, too, with the sun
And gallop on clouds toward Mars.
Then tired of things to the moon we'd beam
And set our clothes on its bay,
Then jump into its sterling streams
And splash a silvery spray.
Or I'd fashion other worlds by hand
While playing on that shore—
And they'd stay the whirling of the sand
As the Zephyrs rolled in roar.
I shine my mirror of innocence
At each new glint of strife;
My mirror I shine with diligence
Each day I pass through life.
I look and ask in wondrous awe
"Who made this world and me?"
Then toddle off—in peace withdraw—

MARVIN JOSAITIS

The skies divert my plea.
I can see a world all made of gold
Just peeping through the dust;
Then I hear the words of wisdom scold,
And babble words of trust.
We're nothing more than little boys,
We're innocence grown wise;
The world around, our faithful toys,
Our garden is the skies.

Being "wonderful" now means that I can continue to find joy in being part of the Josaitis, Girard, Sauvé, and Zelanka heritages interwoven with all the surnames[5] added over time, plus the merging of those from my spouse, Donna: the Rimer, Reau, LaPrad, and Scott heritages, in turn interwoven with others[6]. Looking back is wonderful, but looking forward more wondrous. Donna and I now have the joy of experiencing how each of our children—Kateri, Támara, and Tarik along with Dan, Chris, and Archana (our sons and daughters added along the way)—have retranslated our family traditions in playing old and new music in the fair of life. The mix now includes the Bathgate[7], Gordon[8], and Rao families with all the influences of their ancestral lines.

Our grandchildren, in order of birth, Mackenna Mae Gordon, Cailean Howe Gordon, Talan Rao Josaitis, Adestan Reau Gordon, Jackson William Bathgate, and Eesha Rimer Josaitis—all have family middle names, attesting to the importance and vitality of family. Watching them refashion who we are together, as part of a larger family tradition, they will eventually add more surnames to the

Josaitis' heritage. Watching this unfold will make being "wonderful" something to anticipate with joy.

Fortunately, there also will be pennies from a heav'n that I personally now humbly and gratefully stoop to treasure. It has taken me a long time, but I now truly realize—from the first woman in my life—that pennies from a heav'n continue to appear in my life and in those who will experience the joy of making our family their own.

Endnotes

1   Joyce Carol Oates, *We Were The Mulvaneys*, Penguin, N.Y., N.Y., 1996, pp.3–4.

2   *ibid.*, p.230.

3   Joyce Carol Oates, *We Are The Mulvaneys*, Penguin Press, N.Y., N.Y., 1996, p.437

4   I have written in full about my 12 years of seminary education, ordination to the priesthood, and decision to resign from the priesthood in "Breaking Grand Silence,"(A former Catholic Priest Speaks Out) to be published by Tate Publishing, LLC, Mustang, Oklahoma, in 2011. I have

incorporated some of my family memoire contained herein in that book for complete understanding of who I am.

5 Other 19th century surnames: Ray, Godet, Parent, Labadie, Janis, Navarre, Chene, Meloche, Benoit

6 Other 19th century surnames: Fisher, Raoults, Rau, Valequette, Gee, Shively, Clevenger

7 Other family tree surnames: Allen, Steele, Graham, Sandercock, Proses, Link, Waitson, Hendrikz, Foley

8 Other family tree surnames: May, Howe, Copenhaver, Gray